One Cake, One Hundred Desserts

ONE CAKE,

ONE HUNDRED

DESSERTS

*Learn One Foolproof Cake Recipe
and Make One Hundred Desserts*

Greg Case and Keri Fisher

WM
WILLIAM MORROW
An Imprint of HarperCollins*Publishers*

Insert photographs by Daniel J. van Ackere
Illustrations by Ron Bilodeau
Food styling by Erin McMurrer

ISBN-13: 978-0-06-076535-4

In memory of my mother, Cecelia Jenny Sacci Case, for the love and warmth of her kitchen that nurtured me; to Felipe Rojas-Lombardi, for teaching me the skills and standards to create culinary magic; and to George Roberson, for leading me down the path to Julia Child's door and sharing the high life of NYC in the '80s.

—GC

For the loves of my life: Matty, Declan, and Ronan.

—KF

Contents

Acknowledgments

This book never would have happened without the vision of our agent, Judith Riven, who quickly and expertly guided our proposal from conception to contract, and our editor, Harriet Bell, whose unshakable enthusiasm and responsiveness both delighted and confused us; isn't the publishing world supposed to be vicious and cutthroat? Thanks to Lucy Baker for her patience and persistence and to Carrie Bachman for her drive and dedication.

Thanks to all our tasters and testers: Roz Cummins, Billie Jo Baril, Sarah Benjamin, Cat Palmer, Suzie Hoffer, Jenny Williamson, Jim Smith, Jill Ryder, Rosann Case, Jennie Gilchrist, Devra First, Miriam Dunne, Michelle Tardy, Judith Muska, Vicki Hoffer, Nancy Gifford, Ann Diller, Beth Richman, Judi Fisher, and Heather Hall, and especially to our supertesters, Erika Bruce and Rachel Toomey.

Shooting forty-three cakes in seven days is never easy, and we certainly couldn't have done it without the following people: Everyone at *Cook's Illustrated* and *Cook's Country*, especially Jack Bishop and Chris Kimball, for the generous use of the kitchen, studio, and supplies (we replaced everything we borrowed, we promise!); Garth and Tracey Clingingsmith, who took care of Declan even while days away from the arrival of their own little Dayton; Nadia Domeq for handling all of the shopping; Jason Deneault and Eduardo Lizarraga for loaning us all of their beautiful paper; our gifted photographer, Danny van Ackere, who provided us with both music and mouthwatering images; and most of all, Erin McMurrer, for keeping it all together when we were certain it would all fall apart.

It's a tough job, but someone had to do it, and Marcia, Max, and Corie Walsh, Anthony and

Carrie LaCascia, and everyone at Stone's Public House stepped up to the plate (literally) and ate all the cakes . . . and weren't shy about letting us know what they thought.

We thank (or blame) Cat Palmer for bringing us together, so many years after we all shared the kitchen at Salamander. Thanks to everyone who helped us professionally get where we are today, both through support, advice, and the occasional assignment: John "Doc" Willoughby, Sheryl Julian, Sally Sampson, Barbara Haber, and Jayne Raphael. A very tasty thanks to Nur Kilic for providing us with chocolate and friendship. And we don't know how he did it, but Peter Urban made us look both fabulous and slim, despite excessive cake-eating and advanced pregnancy.

We literally couldn't have done it without KitchenAid, who provided us with a mixer for testing, and Matt Murphy, who provided us with food and liquor (for the cakes!) and made sure none of it went to waste.

To all our friends and family who shared the burden and provided us with support for so many years:

From Greg: To my brother, Ray, and sisters, Rosann and Donna, who gave me support when I chose alternative routes in life; to Jennifer Josephey, the Kellys, Signors, McLaughlins, and Magagnini-Pilkingtons, who, for twenty years, said one day this book would exist; to Alice Fixx for all her wisdom; to Jason Deneault for his love and friendship over the years; and to Keri Fisher, whose talent, humor, and friendship has steered this ship to safe ground.

From Keri: To my sister, Amy Lutz, who may not have tested any recipes (even though she promised she would) but has nonetheless been my strongest advocate and most cutting (and constructive) critic; to my mom, Judi Fisher, who didn't bat an eye when I announced plans to go to cooking school—after I went to "real" college, of course—and has been steadfast in her support through the years; and to Uncle Ronnie, who in my "crazy" days told me I could be anything I wanted to be, and really meant it; to my wonderful husband, Matt Murphy, who reads everything I write with a keen eye and who has been editor, housekeeper, personal chef, and rock throughout this process; and to Greg Case, whose creativity, exuberance, and skill more than made up for his poor sense of time—you are much more than a collaborator, you are a true friend.

And to Glenn Klein, Greg's therapist, who told him, "Just finish the book!" Well, Glenn, we finally did.

One Cake, One Hundred Desserts

Introduction

If you're like most people, you barely have time to brush your teeth, much less to slave in the kitchen making a birthday cake for your daughter or a festive dessert for the holidays. Chances are you have one great dessert that you always make, a dessert you're known for, and when you're invited to parties, people always expect you to bring the same thing. You always think to yourself, "This time I'm going to make something different." But who has time to play around with new recipes, learn new methods, and experiment with new desserts? So when it comes down to it, you stick with what you know. And that dessert is undoubtedly delicious. But what if the one recipe that you knew inside and out gave you a repertoire of one hundred desserts?

Greg is a pastry chef, and almost everything he makes, every dessert he creates, is based upon one or more of a few basic recipes. Many of the cakes that he has sold in his bakeshop, has served at four-star restaurants, or has prepared for dignitaries, celebrities, and friends are based upon one basic sponge cake recipe. His Orange Grand Marnier Upside-Down Cake, Gingerbread Caramel Apple Cake, Apple Charlotte, Frangipane Petits Fours, and Strawberry Bombe are all made with the same basic cake recipe. If you can master one recipe, you can create all of these too, as well as ninety-five other great desserts.

The format of this book is simple. Start at the beginning, with the basic cake recipe. From there, it's up to you. If you're looking for something simple, try one of the pan cakes, which are ready to serve right out of the pan. If you have more time, try an upside-down cake. When it's time to pull out all the stops, make a frosted cake. Add some chocolate to the basic batter and you get a moist, rich chocolate cake that you can fill with chocolate mousse for a decadent Milk Chocolate

Mousse Cake, roll around hazelnut buttercream for a Chocolate Hazelnut Roulade, or top with whipped cream and cherries for a classic Black Forest Cake.

This book is intended for both the committed and the occasional baker. Committed bakers will appreciate the variety of techniques used and will turn to the book not just for recipes but for inspiration. Occasional bakers will appreciate the explicit directions as well as the background information telling them not just the "how" but the "why." Bakers of all levels will be thrilled to master one hundred different desserts.

Most baking books present you with completely new recipes for every cake, insisting that every cake requires a unique formula. But in reality, many cakes are based on a similar core recipe. This book is built on the fact that things are intertwined. Once you learn the techniques, the possibilities are endless.

How to Use This Book

Look at page 12. That's the only cake recipe in this entire book. Really. All the rest of the desserts use that one recipe. Some have other ingredients stirred into the batter, some are layered with frostings or fillings, and some are cut, sliced, or otherwise manipulated so that they don't even look like a cake. But they all start with the same recipe.

There are five steps to the Basic Cake Recipe. By adding different ingredients at one or more steps, you create completely different desserts.

To become comfortable with the one hundred desserts you're about to master, you must first become familiar with the Basic Cake Recipe. So read the recipe through several times so you know what to expect (you should always read a recipe completely before making it).

Ready? Okay, pick a dessert. Read that recipe. It tells you what to add and when to add it. Get your ingredients ready before you begin so you're not running around looking for vanilla while the batter slowly deflates.

Now you're ready to bake.

Tools and Techniques

Having the proper tools and techniques makes any job easier, and baking is no exception. Let our experience be your guide: After years of baking these cakes, we have found that small things can make a big difference.

Bakeware

Nowadays there are many options on the market for bakeware, from flexible silicone to glass. The material you choose will affect the baking time. We highly recommend investing in heavyweight metal pans, which distribute the heat evenly so the cakes bake evenly. Darker bakeware promotes browning and may make the cake bake faster; if you use this kind of bakeware, your cakes will likely be done in the earlier part of the time range given in the recipes. The darker color these pans give the bottom and sides of the cake will not adversely affect their flavor or texture.

ROUND CAKE PANS *Two 9-inch pans, one 10-inch pan* • We recommend straight-sided round cake pans with 2-inch-high sides. The straight sides make for a more attractive cake than sloping ones do, and the higher sides (many cake pans are only 1½ inches high) allow the cake to rise fully without the batter overflowing. Be sure to use the right size pan for each recipe; using a pan that is too big or too small will negatively affect the results. Resist the temptation to use fancy decorative pans or even a Bundt pan; the light nature of the cake means it simply will not work properly in these pans.

SPRINGFORM PAN *One 9-inch pan* • Springform pans have higher sides than regular cake pans (usually about 3 inches high), and the removable ring makes unmolding the cake a snap. We call for springform pans in recipes such as the Cheesecake or Frozen Lemon Soufflé Cake where it might otherwise be difficult, messy, or even damaging to the cake to unmold it from a regular cake pan. Good springform pans can be had for little money, and we think it is worth the investment so a grand cake doesn't fall apart (literally) when you try to unmold it. But though removing the ring from a springform pan is easy, removing the cake from the bottom can be a tricky maneuver. If the cake is sticking, try placing the pan over one of your burners over low heat for about ten seconds to help loosen it. If all else fails, just serve the cake on the springform bottom. No one will notice.

BAKING PAN OR BROWNIE PAN *One 9 by 13-inch pan* • We prefer heavy metal straight-sided pans because the straight sides make for more attractive brownies or bars, but any 9 by 13-inch pan will work in these recipes.

MUFFIN TINS *Two standard 12-cup tins* • Each cup of a standard muffin tin measures 2¾ by 1⅜ inches and has a volume of about ½ cup.

JELLY-ROLL PAN *One 11 by 17-inch pan* • A jelly-roll pan, sometimes called a half sheet pan, is a large baking sheet with sides. Most jelly-roll pans have a standard ½-inch depth. They are a necessity for making, well, jelly rolls and roulades. We also use jelly-roll pans as cookie sheets.

Cookware

The timing in our recipes is based on the size of the cookware used in each recipe; if you substitute a smaller or larger pan, the timing will be off. While this isn't meant to scare you, it is something to be aware of: If you absolutely must use a larger pan, be sure to decrease the amount of time; if you use a smaller pan, you'll likely have to increase the amount of time. While we advocate the use of good-quality heavyweight pots and pans, in these recipes it doesn't make a big difference. Nonstick cookware isn't necessary for any of the recipes, but it won't adversely affect them either. Feel free to use whatever you have on hand.

SMALL SAUCEPAN • When a recipe calls for a small saucepan, we mean a 1-quart saucepan. We use a small saucepan to warm the milk and butter for the cake batter. Because the amounts are small, you want a very small pot so the mixture doesn't quickly boil away.

MEDIUM SAUCEPAN • You'll need a 3- to 4-quart saucepan to make many of the toppings for the upside-down cakes, as well as to serve as the base of an improvised double boiler.

LARGE SKILLET • A 12-inch skillet is essential in several recipes that require a large flat surface to promote evaporation or caramelization.

Smallwares

COOLING RACKS *Two large racks* • Wire cooling racks are necessary to allow for air circulation underneath cake pans, cooling the cake more quickly and evenly. The longer a cake pan stays hot, the longer the cake will continue to bake, which can, in effect, overcook it.

RUBBER SPATULAS • We recommend heat-resistant rubber spatulas, and though they're not necessary for all the cakes, there are instances when they are required (see Caramel Glaze, page 193). We keep several in various sizes on hand. The small ones are great for getting the last bits out of jars, while the bigger ones are ideal for folding batters.

MEASURING CUPS • It's impossible to measure dry ingredients accurately in a liquid measuring cup. That's why it's important to have dry metal or plastic measuring cups as well. You can dip the dry measure in the flour, for example, and level it off.

MEASURING SPOONS • Someday we'll invent a 1½-teaspoon measuring spoon to help us measure the vanilla for this cake, but until then you'll have to suffer with us and use two different measuring spoons for the job. Always level ingredients when measuring them.

MIXING BOWLS *Various sizes* • In general, we prefer wide shallow bowls, which allow for quicker and easier incorporation of ingredients. Make sure you have at least one metal bowl to use as the top of a double boiler. For other uses, the bowl's material usually doesn't matter.

OFFSET/RECESSED SPATULA • We find an offset spatula (also known as a recessed spatula) an absolute necessity. This long, thin, angled spatula makes frosting cakes a breeze, giving you flexibility, leverage, and more control.

Cake Tools

None of these tools are unusual, expensive, or hard to find. Stocking your kitchen does require a small investment, but if you are serious about baking cakes, and other desserts, it's an investment worth making.

Cake Plates

While you don't need cake plates to serve cakes, they do come in handy if you plan on making and serving a lot of them. Greg has been collecting cake plates for years (it's amazing what you can find at thrift stores and yard sales and online) and they can add fun and elegance to the presentation of a cake. Cakes plates should be flat with a low rim or no rim at all; a raised rim can make serving the cake difficult. Covered cake stands are a neat and easy way to protect a cake, especially for frosted cakes, where covering with plastic wrap might ruin the appearance of the cake.

Revolving Cake Stand

Okay, we know that almost no one has a revolving cake stand. But it does make it a lot easier to frost a cake. The idea is that you frost the cake by rotating the cake rather than rotating yourself. You can improvise by placing a flat dinner or serving plate (larger than 9 inches) on top of an inverted bowl with a wide bottom. You can also put a cake plate on a lazy Susan for a similar effect. While you can frost a cake without spinning it, it will be impossible to achieve the decorative swirl we love (see "Frosting a Cake," page 8).

Electric Appliances

ELECTRIC MIXER • While we couldn't live without our KitchenAid stand mixer, we realize that not everyone has one. If you bake a lot, we recommend making the investment; the freedom to do something else while the batter is mixing is priceless, and the ability to use both your hands while the mixer is running (to add the flour to a slowly mixing batter, for example) is a great help. Stand mixers are also more powerful than hand mixers, something to consider if you often mix heavy bread or other doughs. However, a handheld electric mixer will work just as well for the recipes in this book.

Techniques

Baking a cake is easy if you follow a few simple essential techniques. Instead of repeating them in detail throughout the recipes, we've organized them here for easy reference.

PREPARING THE PAN • Greasing and flouring a pan, as opposed to just greasing it, guarantees that your cake will ease right out of it. Here's how to do it: Generously grease the bottom and sides of the pan, using butter or a baking spray such as PAM. Place about 2 tablespoons flour in the pan, pick up the pan, and shake and tap it to distribute the flour evenly over the bottom and sides. Invert the pan over the sink and gently tap it to remove any excess flour. Of course, if you're as lazy as we are, you can skip all this and use baking spray with flour, which is one of the greatest inventions since cake. We love PAM for Baking, which is available in most grocery stores.

Some of these recipes call just for greasing the pan (no flour); in that case you can use butter or regular baking spray. For upside-down cakes with sticky toppings, it's important to use plenty of "grease" so the toppings don't stick when you invert them.

BEATING TO SOFT OR STIFF PEAKS • There are two stages to which you whip egg whites and cream: soft peaks and stiff peaks. Soft peaks means the peaks are literally still soft; when you pull the whisk out of the whipped whites or cream, the peak that comes up will fall back onto itself. Stiff peaks retain their shape completely, pointing straight up when the whisk is lifted out.

FOLDING • Folding is a gentler way of incorporating ingredients than stirring, which can deflate a batter. It's important to do this properly, or you will lose volume in the cake: Insert a rubber spatula into the center of the batter or other mixture, with the flat side facing you, going right to the bottom of the bowl. Drag the spatula toward you and then up the side of the bowl and back toward the center, effectively making a circle through the batter. Rotate the bowl a quarter turn and repeat; repeat around the bowl until the two mixtures or ingredients are just combined.

MELTING CHOCOLATE • Chocolate melts at a low temperature, and if it's exposed to high heat it can easily burn, which is why chocolate should never be melted over direct heat. Instead, use an indirect-heat method, like a double boiler, or the microwave. To melt chocolate in a double boiler, place the chopped chocolate in a heat-resistant bowl set over a pot of barely simmering water; the bottom of the bowl should not touch the water. Stir occasionally with a spatula until the chocolate is melted. To melt chocolate in the microwave, place the chopped chocolate in a microwave-safe bowl. To avoid "cooking" the chocolate, set the microwave for increments of 20 seconds, and stir after each interval. Don't be fooled if the chocolate looks solid; chocolate melted in the microwave will hold its shape until you stir it (even if it's completely melted).

Chocolate sets quickly as it cools, so be sure to wait until you need it before melting it.

ROLLING A ROULADE • Using a dish towel helps you roll up a roulade cake neatly and evenly. After applying the filling in an even layer, gently roll up the cake, using the dish towel to lift the cake and using your fingers to tuck in the edge. Roll the cake tightly, ending with the seam side down, and use the towel to help press the cake into an even roll. Remove the dish towel and use one or two large spatulas to transfer the roulade to a serving platter.

LINING THE BOWL FOR A BOMBE • First cut out a circle of cake that will just fit inside the top of the bowl; this will be the bottom of the bombe when it is turned out. Then cut the remaining cake into pieces to line the bowl, following the diagram. Lay the square pieces in the bowl first: Place one in the bottom center of the bowl, then place one square against each straight edge of the bottom square. Place a triangular piece in each of the remaining spaces, without overlapping the pieces. Trim any excess that comes above the rim of the bowl. You will have some cake left for snacking.

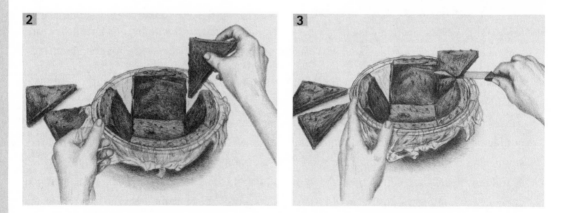

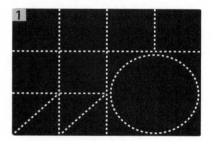

FROSTING A CAKE • To keep things tidy while frosting a cake, first place four strips of wax paper underneath the cake at intersecting angles, so that there is wax paper all around the edges of the cake. This will keep excess frosting off the cake plate; then the wax paper strips can be removed, frosting and all, when you are finished. (And you can lick the frosting off the wax paper.)

To frost the cake: Spoon about half of the frosting onto the center of the top of the cake. Using the flat bottom of an offset spatula, spread the frosting from the center to the edges of the cake, letting some come over the sides and rotating the cake as you go to ensure even coverage. The goal is a thick (about ¼-inch), even layer of frosting on top of the cake, with plenty extending beyond the edges and down the sides.

Again using the bottom of the offset spatula, scoop some frosting out of the bowl and spread it along the side of the cake, holding the spatula vertical and parallel to the side of the cake and slowly spinning the cake as you apply the frosting in an even layer. Repeat with the remaining frosting to cover the sides completely.

Once the cake is completely covered with frosting, you need to even and polish it. Holding the clean, dry offset spatula vertically, with the bottom against the side of the cake, drag the spatula around the cake, applying steady pressure and scraping off any excess frosting. As you

even and smooth the frosting with this technique, a slight raised lip should form along the top edge of the cake.

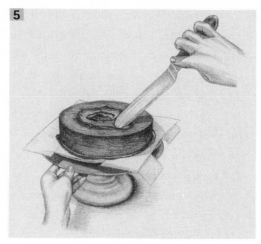

Scrape the spatula on the side of the bowl to remove the excess frosting. Now, hold the spatula horizontally, with the bottom parallel to the top of the cake and about 1 inch away from the edge of the cake, gently push the lip of frosting about 2 inches toward the center of the cake, smoothing the edges as you do so. Scrape the spatula on the side of the bowl to remove any excess frosting, and repeat around the entire cake.

To add a decorative swirl: With the tip of the offset spatula, place a small dollop of frosting in the center of the cake. Pressing down with the tip of the spatula, slowly pull the frosting out in a spiral as you spin the cake, stopping when you get to the outer edge of the cake.

MAKING DECORATIVE CHOCOLATE SHAVINGS AND CURLS • Chocolate shavings are a nice finishing touch for many chocolate desserts and a traditional finish to desserts such as tiramisu. To make shavings, hold a piece of chocolate (the thicker it is, the easier this will be) over the cake and run it over a fine-toothed grater (like a Microplane, or the small holes of a box grater). Avoid handling the shavings, as the heat from your hands will melt the chocolate.

For chocolate curls, run a vegetable peeler over the side of a thick piece of room-temperature chocolate. These chocolate "peelings" are thin and will curl naturally.

The Cake

We love this cake for its simplicity, its versatility, and, most important, its taste. After all, what good is a cake you can use to create one hundred different desserts if it doesn't taste good to begin with? This cake tastes great plain, sprinkled with confectioners' sugar, squirted with lemon juice, or drizzled with hot fudge. And when the urge to bake strikes at 11:30 on a Sunday night, odds are that you'll have all the ingredients you need in your pantry and refrigerator.

This cake is what is called a hot milk sponge cake, a type of egg foam cake—a large amount of the leavening (what makes it rise) comes from air that is beaten into the eggs, as opposed to the leavening in a butter cake or a pound cake, where air is beaten into butter. Other egg foam cakes include chiffon, angel food, and génoise, as well as regular sponge cake. Some egg foam cakes, like génoise, use air as the only leavening agent, which can be a bit risky—if there's not enough air in the batter, the cake will fall. The hot milk sponge cake uses both air and baking powder, which makes it practically foolproof.

In baking, the term "crumb" is used to describe the texture of a cake—the larger the crumb, the coarser the texture. This cake has a fine, light, airy crumb. It's soft and buttery. It's delicate to eat but surprisingly sturdy and easy to handle, which is very important when making many of the desserts in this book.

And let's not forget the very premise upon which the book is based: This is an incredibly versatile cake. The flavor is neutral and clean, so it lends itself well to taking on other flavors. While it's a good cake in and of itself, it's also able to take on many other guises.

BASIC CAKE RECIPE

Six minutes may seem like a long time to whisk eggs, but there's a good reason: Beating builds strength in the protein in the eggs, so when you fold in the other ingredients, like flour, the eggs can support the addition without losing air and deflating. And there are specific reasons for all the steps used in making this cake. Lowering the mixer speed halfway through mixing prevents the incorporated air from escaping. Combining the warm milk and butter and the batter in stages is important, because if you pour the entire hot milk mixture directly into all of the batter, it will sink to the bottom of the bowl and be difficult to incorporate evenly.

Be sure to read through the entire recipe before making the cake for the first time so you know what to expect after each step. While this batter is used in many different ways for the recipes in the book, here we provide instructions for baking a 9-inch round cake.

To serve, sprinkle with confectioners' sugar, or dress it up with Hot Fudge Sauce (page 195), Caramel Glaze (page 193), or Whipped Cream (page 197) and fresh berries. **Serves 8 to 10**

Baking spray with flour or unsalted butter and all-purpose flour for the pan

¾ cup all-purpose flour

1 teaspoon baking powder

¼ cup milk

2 tablespoons unsalted butter, cut into 2 pieces

1½ teaspoons vanilla extract

3 large eggs, at room temperature

3 large egg yolks, at room temperature

¾ cup sugar

To bake a 9-inch cake: Preheat the oven to 350°F and position a rack in the center. Grease and flour a 9-inch round cake pan.

1. Combine the flour and baking powder in a large bowl, and set aside.

2. Heat the milk and butter in a small saucepan over low heat. As soon as the butter is melted, remove from the heat and add the vanilla. Set aside.

3. Using the whisk attachment of a stand mixer (or, if using a hand mixer, the regular beaters), whip the eggs, egg yolks, and sugar in the large mixer bowl (or other large bowl) on high speed for 3 minutes. The mixture will triple in volume and turn a very pale yellow. Reduce the speed to medium and continue whipping for 3 minutes (if using a hand mixer, keep the speed at high). The mixture will continue to increase in volume and thicken.

4. With the mixer on the lowest speed, slowly sprinkle ¼ cup of the flour mixture over the eggs and mix until no trace of white remains. Repeat with the remaining flour mixture in 2 additions; reserve the empty flour bowl. When the flour is fully incorporated, the batter will be thick and stiff; if you let it pour off the whisk into the bowl, it will fall back on itself like a ribbon.

5. Pour half of the batter into the empty flour bowl. Pour the warm milk mixture into the batter and stir gently to combine. Slowly pour the milk/batter mixture back into the mixing bowl, and using a rubber spatula, fold the mixtures together quickly but gently until fully blended. You will see tiny air bubbles appear on the surface; work quickly to prevent too much air from escaping.

6. To bake the cake, pour the batter into the prepared pan and place on the center rack of the oven. Bake for 30 to 40 minutes, or until the edges pull back from the pan and a toothpick inserted in the center of the cake comes out clean. Set the cake on a rack to cool.

7. When the cake is cool, run a knife around the edge of the pan and turn the cake out onto a plate, then use a cake plate to flip the cake again so it is right side up.

Pan Cakes

No, not the kind you serve with syrup, these are cakes that you serve right out of the pan—no fuss, no mess. These are the simplest cakes in the book, but sometimes the most transformed. Add some melted chocolate, and the cake goes from light and fluffy to moist and dense. Fold in cream cheese, and the sponge cake becomes a rich, creamy cheesecake.

These self-contained cakes are quick and easy, with a lot of variety. Just a few minor changes to the basic cake and you've got an incredible variety of desserts, from basic blueberry to anything-but-ordinary Caribbean Rum Raisin.

These recipes will become your standards, the ones you can pull together on a moment's notice when company's coming. With only one pan, there's little cleanup to worry about, and with just a few steps, you won't have to worry about spending all afternoon in the kitchen.

These cakes generally travel well, so they are also good for picnics and bake sales. Wrapped well, they will keep for about 3 days at room temperature.

Apple Spice Cake

We love this cake warm from the oven (or you can cheat and microwave a cold piece for 10 seconds), a perfect afternoon snack on a cold autumn afternoon. Though it is quite plain in appearance, the rich, earthy spices and the moist applesauce give this humble cake great flavor and depth. To dress it up, serve with Whipped Cream (page 197) and Caramel Glaze (page 193). **Serves 8 to 10**

Baking spray with flour or unsalted butter and
    all-purpose flour for the pan

1 Basic Cake Recipe (page 12), minus the granulated sugar

½ teaspoon ground cinnamon

¼ teaspoon ground cloves

¼ teaspoon ground nutmeg

¼ teaspoon ground allspice

¾ cup packed dark brown sugar

⅔ cup applesauce

Preheat the oven to 350°F and position a rack in the center. Grease and flour a 9-inch round cake pan.

Prepare the batter according to the recipe, with the following changes: In Step 1, add the spices to the flour and baking powder. In Step 3, replace the granulated sugar with the dark brown sugar. In Step 5, quickly but gently fold the applesauce into the finished batter until just combined.

Pour the batter into the prepared pan. Bake for 30 to 40 minutes, until the edges pull back from the pan and a toothpick inserted in the center of the cake comes out clean. Set the cake on a rack to cool for 10 minutes.

Run a knife around the edge of the pan and turn the cake out onto a plate, then use a cake plate to flip the cake again so it is right side up. Serve warm.

Biscotti Cake

Originally this was going to be called Anise-Almond Cake, but once we made it, we knew we had to change the name. The crisp crust on the cake and the heady aroma of anise evoked images of crowded cafés in Italy—and biscotti, which are traditionally flavored with anise and almond. This is a great break- fast cake, simple to make but complex and distinct in flavor, and its crisp crust contrasts with the soft, fluffy interior. Toast slices of it if you like.

   Be careful when grinding the almonds—if you process them too long, the oils will be released and the nuts will turn to almond butter. **Serves 8 to 10**

Baking spray or butter for the pan

1¼ cups (4½ ounces) sliced almonds

½ teaspoon whole aniseed

1 Basic Cake Recipe (page 12)

½ teaspoon ground aniseed

Preheat the oven to 350°F and position a rack in the center. Generously grease a 9-inch round cake pan.

Combine ¼ cup of the sliced almonds and the whole aniseed and crush the almonds coarsely with your hands. Place in the prepared pan and turn and tilt to coat the pan bottom and sides evenly.

Grind the remaining 1 cup almonds in a food processor until fine, about 20 seconds; take care not to overprocess.

Prepare the cake batter according to the recipe, with the following change: In Step 1, add the ground almonds and ground aniseed to the flour mixture.

Pour the batter into the prepared pan. Bake for 30 to 40 minutes, until the edges pull back from the pan and a toothpick inserted in the center of the cake comes out clean. Set the cake on a rack to cool.

When the cake is cool, run a knife around the edge of the pan and turn the cake out onto a cake plate. Serve at room temperature.

Blueberry Cake

We love this cake for its simple country charm. Moist, light, and delicious, studded with burst blueberries, it has that fresh-fruit-out-of-the-garden flavor (even when you use frozen blueberries). The lemon rounds out the sweetness of the berries with a little tanginess. This cake is at home in all kinds of settings—at the breakfast table, on a picnic, sliced and topped with ice cream. And it is the perfect choice for a lunch box. **Serves 8 to 10**

*Baking spray with flour or unsalted butter
    and all-purpose flour for the pan*

Ingredients for Basic Cake Recipe (page 12)

2 teaspoons grated lemon zest

8 ounces fresh or unthawed frozen blueberries

1 tablespoon all-purpose flour

2 tablespoons sugar

1 teaspoon ground cinnamon

Preheat the oven to 350°F and position a rack in the center. Grease and flour a 9-inch round cake pan.

Prepare the batter according to the recipe, with the following change: In Step 2, stir the lemon zest into the warm milk and butter.

Pour the batter into the prepared pan. Place the blueberries in a medium bowl, sprinkle with the flour, sugar, and cinnamon, and toss until the blueberries are evenly coated. Pour the blueberries on top of the cake batter. The batter is very thick, so the blueberries will just sit on top—at first. As it bakes, the berries will sink into the cake.

Bake for 30 to 40 minutes, until the edges pull back from the pan and a toothpick inserted in the center of the cake comes out clean. Set the cake on a rack to cool for 10 minutes.

Run a knife around the edge of the pan and turn the cake out onto a plate, then use a cake plate to flip the cake again so it is right side up. Serve warm or at room temperature, plain or with Lemon Curd (page 185) and/or Whipped Cream (page 197).

Caribbean Rum Raisin Cake

Rum and raisins are a classic pairing, the spiciness of the Caribbean rum offsetting the intense sweetness of the raisins. We add more Caribbean flavor with the nutmeg and molasses (in the brown sugar). The key to the cake is soaking the raisins in rum, which not only adds intense rum flavor, but also makes even shriveled raisins plump and moist. **Serves 8 to 10**

½ cup dark rum

1 cup raisins

*Baking spray with flour or unsalted butter and
    all-purpose flour for the pan*

1 Basic Cake Recipe (page 12), minus the granulated sugar

¼ teaspoon ground nutmeg

¾ cup packed light brown sugar

Combine the rum and raisins in a small bowl and let soak for 30 minutes.

Preheat the oven to 350°F and position a rack in the center. Grease and flour a 9-inch round cake pan.

Transfer the raisins and rum to a food processor and process until the raisins are coarsely chopped, about 15 seconds.

Prepare the batter according to the recipe, with the following changes: In Step 1, add the nutmeg to the flour and baking powder. In Step 3, replace the granulated sugar with the light brown sugar. In Step 5, quickly but gently fold the raisin mixture into the finished batter until just combined.

Pour the batter into the prepared pan. Bake for 30 to 40 minutes, until the edges pull back from the pan and a toothpick inserted in the center of the cake comes out clean. Set the cake on a rack to cool.

When the cake is cool, run a knife around the edge of the pan and turn the cake out onto a plate, then use a cake plate to flip the cake again so it is right side up. Serve at room temperature. (The cake is also good warm, but the flavors are more pronounced once it has cooled to room temperature.)

Chai Cake

This cake was inspired by Keri's daily forays into Starbucks for the latte of the moment. *Chai* means tea in Hindi, and traditionally it refers to a blend of tea and spices that include cinnamon, cloves, cardamom, and ginger. The sweet, heady aroma and warm flavors make it a natural for the American palate. To make powdered chai, empty several chai teabags into a spice grinder and grind until powdery. A little bit goes a long way. **Serves 8 to 10**

*Baking spray with flour or unsalted butter
    and all-purpose flour for the pan*

1 Basic Cake Recipe (page 12)

1 teaspoon powdered chai (see headnote)

Preheat the oven to 350°F and position a rack in the center. Grease and flour a 9-inch round cake pan.

Prepare the cake batter according to the recipe, with the following change: In Step 2, add the chai to the warm milk and butter and stir to dissolve (the mixture will thicken somewhat).

Pour the batter into the prepared pan. Bake for 30 to 40 minutes, until the edges pull back from the pan and a toothpick inserted in the center of the cake comes out clean. Set the cake on a rack to cool for 10 minutes.

Run a knife around the edge of the pan and turn the cake out onto a plate, then use a cake plate to flip it again so it is right side up. Serve warm or at room temperature.

Cheesecake

This is one of our favorite cakes in the book, combining the creamy richness of New York cheesecake with a slightly cakey texture. This cake is baked, like a custard, in a water bath, which creates a buffer against the direct oven heat so the cake cooks slowly and evenly. Make sure you use hot water for the water bath; if the water bath isn't hot going into the oven, it will take longer for the cake to cook. Like any cheesecake, this one must set overnight, or for at least 8 hours, in the refrigerator, so plan accordingly. **Serves 10 to 12**

Baking spray or butter for the pan

5 ounces graham crackers (about 1 sleeve, or 10 whole crackers)

4 tablespoons unsalted butter, melted

12 ounces cream cheese, at room temperature

½ cup sugar

1 Basic Cake Recipe (page 12)

Preheat the oven to 350°F and position a rack in the center. Grease a 9-inch springform pan. Wrap the bottom and sides of the pan in a double layer of aluminum foil to prevent leaks (even the best springform pans can leak a bit).

Process the graham crackers in a food processor until finely ground, about 30 seconds (if any large pieces remain, break them up with your fingers and then pulse a few more times). Add the butter and pulse 3 to 5 times, until the mixture resembles wet sand. Pour into the prepared pan and shake to distribute the crumbs evenly, then press them into a compact, even layer with your fingers or the bottom of a metal measuring cup.

Bake the crust for 10 minutes, or until lightly browned. Set on a rack to cool. (Leave the oven on.)

Place the cream cheese and sugar in a large bowl and stir until well blended.

Prepare the cake batter according to the recipe. Add about 1 cup of the batter to the cream cheese mixture and stir until combined. Add half the remaining batter to the cream cheese mixture and gently fold to combine. Fold in the remaining batter.

Pour the batter into the prepared pan. Place the pan in a large pan, such as a roasting pan, and fill the larger pan with hot water to come about halfway up the sides of the springform pan. Bake for 65 to 70 minutes, until all but the very center of the cake is set (the center should jiggle slightly when the pan is shaken). If the top looks dark before the cake is set, cover the cake loosely with aluminum foil to prevent overbrowning.

Remove the cake from the oven and let it sit in the water bath for 15 minutes. Remove the cake from the water, remove the foil wrapping (be careful, as water tends to collect inside the foil), and set the cake on a rack. Run a knife around the edge of the pan to release the cake, but do not remove the ring.

Allow the cake to cool, then refrigerate for at least 8 hours, or overnight, until chilled and completely set. Remove from the refrigerator and let sit at room temperature for 30 minutes before removing the ring and serving.

Serve plain, or topped with a thick layer of Lemon Curd (page 185), coated with Chocolate Glaze (page 194), or drizzled with Strawberry Sauce (page 196).

Chocolate Tweed Cake

The frugal European tradition of making use of every item of food inspired this recipe. Instead of being thrown away, stale bread was often ground and used as a substitute for flour. Here the savory quality of pumpernickel bread adds a unique flavor to the sweet chocolate cake. You won't taste the pumpernickel, it just accents the chocolate.

Where does the name come from? We think the baked cake looks like tweed, with the chocolate cake speckled with crumbs of dark brown bread. **Serves 8 to 10**

*Baking spray with flour or unsalted butter and
    all-purpose flour for the pan*

1 Basic Cake Recipe (page 12)

2 slices pumpernickel bread, stale or toasted

4 ounces semisweet chocolate, chopped

Preheat the oven to 350°F and position a rack in the center. Grease and flour a 9-inch round cake pan.

Prepare the cake batter according to the recipe, with the following changes: In Step 1, reduce the amount of flour to ½ cup. Place the flour, baking powder, bread, and chocolate chips in a food processor. Process until the mixture is fine and uniform and resembles chocolate flour, about 30 seconds.

Pour the batter into the prepared pan. Bake for 30 to 40 minutes, until the edges pull back from the pan and a toothpick inserted in the center of the cake comes out clean. Set the cake on a rack to cool for 10 minutes.

Run a knife around the edge of the pan and turn the cake out onto a plate, then use a cake plate to flip it again so it is right side up. Serve warm or at room temperature (the flavors will be more pronounced at room temperature), with Whipped Cream (page 197), or toast slices and serve with jam.

Coconut Cake

The toasted coconut on the top of the cake becomes a deliciously crunchy crust that yields to the soft cake beneath. Lemon brings out the flavor of the coconut, just as salt brings out the flavor of savory foods. With its coarse crumb and not-too-sweet taste, this cake is perfect for backyard barbecues and picnics. **Serves 8 to 10**

*Baking spray with flour or unsalted butter and
    all-purpose flour for the pan*

2 cups sweetened shredded coconut

1 Basic Cake Recipe (page 12)

2 tablespoons fresh lemon juice

Preheat the oven to 350°F and position a rack in the center. Grease and flour a 9-inch round cake pan.

Spread the coconut in an even layer on a baking sheet and toast for 8 to 10 minutes, until lightly browned, with some white spots. Place on a rack to cool.

Spread ½ cup of the toasted coconut in an even layer in the bottom of the prepared pan. Grind the remaining coconut in a food processor until fine, about 30 seconds.

Prepare the cake batter according to the recipe, with the following changes: In Step 1, add the ground coconut to the flour mixture. In Step 2, add the lemon juice with the vanilla.

Pour the batter into the prepared pan. Bake for 30 to 40 minutes, until the edges pull back from the pan and a toothpick inserted in the center of the cake comes out clean. Set the cake on a rack to cool.

When the cake is cool, run a knife around the edge of the pan and turn the cake out onto a plate, then use a cake plate to flip the cake again so it is right side up. Serve with Whipped Cream (page 197), flavored with rum, and/or sliced fresh tropical fruit, such as pineapple or kiwi.

Fig Ouzo Cake

Ouzo is a Greek anise-flavored liqueur, and its spicy licorice flavor is a perfect complement to the earthy sweetness of figs. Poaching the dried figs in ouzo and water softens, tenderizes, and flavors them. The poached figs are almost jellylike in texture, dotted with the crunch of tiny seeds. The moist figs are placed atop the batter before it goes into the oven, and as it bakes, they travel down through the batter to the bottom of the cake, leaving behind a syrupy licorice trail. The cake is inverted when served, so the bottom becomes the top, studded with sweet, juicy fruit. Be sure to use Black Mission figs, which have a richer flavor and better texture than other varieties. **Serves 8 to 10**

*Baking spray with flour or unsalted butter and
    all-purpose flour for the pan*

8 ounces dried Black Mission figs, stemmed and halved

*¼ cup plus 1 tablespoon ouzo, sambuca, or
    other anise-flavored liqueur*

1 Basic Cake Recipe (page 12)

Preheat the oven to 350°F and position a rack in the center. Grease and flour a 9-inch round cake pan.

Place the figs, ¼ cup of the ouzo, and ½ cup water in a small saucepan over medium-high heat and bring to a boil. Reduce the heat to low, cover the saucepan, and simmer until almost all the liquid is absorbed (you will see just a thin smear of liquid on the bottom of the pan), about 20 minutes. Transfer to a bowl and refrigerate until ready to use.

Prepare the cake batter according to the recipe, with the following change: In Step 2, add the remaining 1 tablespoon ouzo with the vanilla.

Pour the batter into the prepared pan and drop the figs evenly atop the batter (they will sink). Bake for 30 to 40 minutes, until the edges pull away from the pan and a toothpick inserted in the center of the cake comes out clean. Set the cake on a rack to cool.

When the cake is cool, run a knife around the edge of the pan and turn the cake out onto a cake plate. Serve plain or with Whipped Cream (page 197).

Gingerbread

Gingerbread was once a treat because spices were so rare and expensive. Though spices are now plentiful and many people take gingerbread for granted these days, we still think it's a treat. Unlike traditional dense gingerbread, our version is light and fluffy. But, like traditional gingerbread, it features warm wintry spices that make it the perfect snack on a cold, gray day. **Serves 10 to 12**

Baking spray with flour or unsalted butter and
all-purpose flour for the pan

1 Basic Cake Recipe (page 12), minus ½ cup of the sugar

2 teaspoons ground ginger

½ teaspoon ground cinnamon

¼ teaspoon ground allspice

¼ cup unsulphured (mild) molasses

½ cup packed dark brown sugar

Preheat the oven to 350°F and position a rack in the center. Grease and flour a 9 by 13-inch baking pan.

Prepare the cake batter according to the recipe, with the following changes: In Step 1, add the ginger, cinnamon, and allspice to the flour mixture. In Step 2, add the molasses to the warm milk and butter and stir to dissolve. In Step 3, replace ½ cup of the granulated sugar with the dark brown sugar.

Pour the batter into the prepared pan. Bake for 15 to 18 minutes, until the edges pull back from the pan and a toothpick inserted in the center of the cake comes out clean. Set the cake on a rack to cool slightly.

Cut the cake into squares, still in the pan. Serve warm with hot applesauce or Whipped Cream (page 197).

Honey Sesame Cake

Glistening with honey and dotted with crunchy sesame seeds, this is one of the most beautiful cakes in the book. It's also one of the most delicious. The nutty sesame seeds offset the sweet richness of the honey while adding a crunchy crust. We use local honey for this cake (make friends with a local beekeeper at a farmers' market). Remember that different honeys add different flavors, so experiment to find out which one you like best. We prefer the delicate flavor of orange blossom honey or the light-tasting alfalfa honey. Toasting the sesame seeds brings out their flavor and makes them even crunchier. **Serves 8 to 10**

Baking spray or butter for the pan

⅓ cup white sesame seeds

1 Basic Cake Recipe (page 12)

½ cup honey

Preheat the oven to 350°F and position a rack in the center. Generously grease a 9-inch round cake pan.

Toast the sesame seeds in a small skillet over medium heat until lightly browned and aromatic, 5 to 7 minutes.

Place the sesame seeds in the prepared pan and turn and tilt the pan to coat the bottom and sides evenly.

Prepare the batter according to the recipe.

Pour the batter into the prepared pan and bake for 30 to 40 minutes, until the edges pull back from the pan and a toothpick inserted in the center of the cake comes out clean. Set the cake on a rack to cool for 10 minutes.

Run a knife around the edge of the pan and turn the cake out onto a cake plate. Melt the honey in the microwave or in a small saucepan over medium heat. Pour the warm honey onto the center of the cake and, working quickly, swirl and turn the cake to coat it evenly with honey, using an offset spatula to spread the honey to the edges and allowing some to drip down the sides. Let cool.

Serve at room temperature. (Do not refrigerate or freeze this cake; the crisp exterior will become soggy.)

Key Lime Cheesecake

Key limes take their name from the Florida Keys, the string of small islands off the southeast coast of the state. Because the Keys were so isolated before the railroad was opened in 1912, fresh milk was in short supply. Luckily there was sweetened condensed milk for making sweet, creamy custards and cheesecakes. Key limes are both expensive and tiny—you have to squeeze a lot of them to get enough juice for a cake—so we use a combination of regular limes and lemons to approximate their sweet-tart flavor.

Be sure to wash the mixing bowl thoroughly after making the Key lime mixture—if there are any traces of it left in the bowl, the eggs for the cake batter will not whip properly. And use hot water for the water bath; if the water bath isn't hot going into the oven, it will take longer for the cake to cook.

Like any cheesecake, this one must set overnight, or for at least 8 hours, in the refrigerator, so plan accordingly. **Serves 10 to 12**

Baking spray or butter for the pan

5 ounces graham crackers (about 1 sleeve, or 10 whole crackers)

4 tablespoons unsalted butter, melted

2 large eggs

3 large egg yolks

One 14-ounce can sweetened condensed milk

1 tablespoon grated lime zest

½ cup fresh lime juice

¼ cup fresh lemon juice

1 Basic Cake Recipe (page 12)

Preheat the oven to 325°F and position a rack in the center. Grease a 9-inch springform pan. Wrap the bottom and sides of the pan in a double layer of aluminum foil to prevent leaks (even the best springform pans can leak a bit).

Process the graham crackers in a food processor until finely ground, about 30 seconds (if any large pieces remain, break them up with your fingers and then pulse a few more times). Add the melted butter and pulse 3 to 5 times, or until the mixture resembles wet sand. Pour into the prepared pan and shake to distribute the crumbs evenly, then press them into a compact, even layer with your fingers or the bottom of a metal measuring cup.

Bake the crust for 10 minutes, or until browned. Set on a rack to cool. (Leave the oven on.)

Combine the eggs, egg yolks, and condensed milk in the bowl of a stand mixer and beat at high speed for 4 minutes; the mixture will be light and fluffy. You can also use a handheld mixer if necessary. With the mixer on low speed, add the lime zest, lime juice, and lemon juice and mix until just combined. Transfer the mixture to another large bowl and wash the mixer bowl before preparing the cake batter.

Prepare the batter according to the recipe. Add the batter to the lime mixture and fold together quickly but gently.

Pour the batter into the prepared pan. Place the pan in a larger pan, such as a roasting pan, and fill the larger pan with hot water to come about halfway up the sides of the springform pan. Bake for 70 to 75 minutes, until all but the very center of the cake is set (the center should jiggle slightly when the pan is shaken). Turn off the oven and leave the cake inside to set 15 minutes longer.

Remove the cake from the water bath, remove the foil wrapping (be careful, as water tends to collect inside the foil), and set it on a rack. Run a knife around the edge of the pan to release the cake, but do not remove the ring.

Allow the cake to cool, then refrigerate for at least 8 hours, or overnight, until chilled and completely set. Remove from the refrigerator and let sit at room temperature for 30 minutes before removing the ring and serving.

Lemon Poppy Seed Cake

This is a great cake for afternoon tea. The acidity of the lemon juice rounds out the slightly licorice flavor of the poppy seeds, and we bring out that flavor even more by toasting them, giving them a smoky, nutty flavor and excellent crunch. And the lemon glaze guarantees a moist texture. **Serves 8 to 10**

Baking spray with flour or unsalted butter and
   all-purpose flour for the pan

2 tablespoons poppy seeds

1 Basic Cake Recipe (page 12)

For the glaze

¼ cup fresh lemon juice

½ cup sugar

Preheat the oven to 350°F and position a rack in the center. Grease and flour a 9-inch round cake pan.

Toast the poppy seeds in a small skillet over medium-high heat until dark and aromatic, 2 to 4 minutes. Let cool.

Prepare the cake batter according to the recipe, with the following change: In Step 1, add the poppy seeds to the flour.

Pour the batter into the prepared pan. Bake for 30 to 40 minutes, until the edges pull back from the pan and a toothpick inserted in the center of the cake comes out clean. Set the cake on a rack to cool for 10 minutes.

While the cake is cooling, prepare the glaze: Combine the lemon juice and sugar in a small saucepan and bring to a boil over medium-high heat. Cook for 1 minute, stirring occasionally. Remove from the heat.

Run a knife around the edge of the pan and turn the cake out onto a cake plate. Using a pastry brush, spread the glaze evenly over the top and sides of the cake (the glaze will quickly be absorbed into the cake). Let cool before serving.

Maple Walnut Cake

This is a classic New England cake, pairing the sweetness of maple syrup with the slight bitterness of walnuts. We use Grade B maple syrup, which is more intense than the more popular Grade A. To boost the maple flavor even more, we replace some of the granulated sugar in the batter with dark brown sugar. **Serves 8 to 10**

*Baking spray with flour, or unsalted butter and
all-purpose flour for the pan*

1 Basic Cake Recipe (page 12), minus ½ cup of the sugar

¾ cup chopped walnuts

½ cup maple syrup, preferably Grade B

½ cup packed dark brown sugar

Preheat the oven to 350°F and position a rack in the center. Grease and flour a 9-inch round cake pan.

Prepare the cake batter according to the recipe, with the following changes: In Step 1, process the walnuts in a food processor until coarsely ground, about 15 seconds. Add the flour and baking powder and pulse to combine. In Step 2, add the maple syrup to the warm milk and butter and stir to dissolve. In Step 3, replace ½ cup of the granulated sugar with the dark brown sugar.

Pour the batter into the prepared pan. Bake for 30 to 40 minutes, until the edges pull back from the pan and a toothpick inserted in the center of the cake comes out clean. Set the cake on a rack to cool slightly.

Run a knife around the edge of the pan and turn the cake out onto a plate, then use a cake plate to flip the cake again so it is right side up. Serve warm.

Marble Cake

This cake offers the best of both worlds. It's great when you can't decide if you want chocolate or vanilla—you get some of both. It's also great when you want a really beautiful dessert: the cake is a cinch to make, and the glaze gives it a polished, refined finish. **Serves 8**

Baking spray with flour or unsalted butter and
    all-purpose flour for the pan

1 Basic Cake Recipe (page 12)

½ cup cocoa powder, whisked to remove lumps

For the white glaze

1 large egg white

1¼ cups confectioners' sugar

For the chocolate glaze

1 ounce semisweet chocolate, chopped

1 tablespoon unsalted butter

Preheat the oven to 350°F and position a rack in the center. Grease and flour a 9-inch round cake pan.

Prepare the cake batter according to the recipe. Transfer one-quarter of the batter to another bowl, and add the cocoa in two batches, stirring well after each addition, until completely combined and no streaks remain. Add the chocolate batter to the remaining batter and fold it in with only two strokes of the spatula, so that the chocolate is streaked throughout the white batter.

Pour the batter into the prepared pan. Bake for 30 to 40 minutes, until the edges pull back from the pan and a toothpick inserted in the center of the cake comes out clean. Set the cake on a rack to cool.

When the cake is cool, run a knife around the edge of the pan and turn the cake out onto a plate, then use a cake plate to flip the cake again so it is right side up.

Prepare the glazes: Combine the egg white and confectioners' sugar in the bowl of a stand mixer and mix on medium speed just until smooth, about 10 seconds; do not overmix—you don't want to incorporate too much air. Melt the chocolate and butter in the microwave or in a double boiler and stir to combine.

Pour the white glaze onto the center of the cake. Using an offset spatula, spread the glaze evenly over the top of the cake, allowing it to drip down the sides. Working quickly, drop spoonfuls of the chocolate glaze evenly over the top of the cake, again allowing some to drip down the sides. Using a toothpick, swirl the chocolate glaze into the white glaze, creating a marbled effect. Let stand at room temperature until the glaze is set and no longer tacky, about 1 hour, before serving. (Do not refrigerate this cake; the moisture will cause the glaze to sweat.)

Mexican Chocolate Cake

Traditional Mexican hot chocolate—strong and rich, with a hint of spice and almonds—inspired this cake. It's moist and fudgy, with a crisp brownielike top. Serves 8 to 10

Baking spray with flour, or unsalted butter and
all-purpose flour for the pan

1½ teaspoons ground cinnamon

⅛ teaspoon cayenne pepper

¾ cup (about 3 ounces) sliced almonds

1 Basic Cake Recipe (page 12)

8 ounces semisweet chocolate, chopped

Preheat the oven to 350°F and position a rack in the center. Grease and flour a 9-inch round cake pan.

Combine the cinnamon, cayenne, and almonds in a small skillet over medium-high heat and toast until the almonds begin to brown and the spices are aromatic, 5 to 7 minutes. Transfer to a plate to cool.

Prepare the cake batter according to the recipe, with the following changes: In Step 1, grind the almonds in a food processor until fine. Add the flour and baking powder and pulse until combined. In Step 5, melt the chocolate in a large bowl in the microwave, or melt the chocolate in a double boiler and then transfer it to a large bowl (this must be done at the last minute so the chocolate doesn't set). Add the warm milk and butter to the chocolate and stir until combined, then add half the cake batter to the chocolate. Stir quickly but gently until the chocolate is evenly distributed. Gently fold the chocolate batter into the remaining batter until completely combined and no streaks remain.

Pour the batter into the prepared pan. Bake for 30 to 40 minutes, until the edges pull back from the pan and a toothpick inserted in the center of the cake comes out with a few moist crumbs but is not wet. Set the cake on a rack to cool slightly.

Run a knife around the edge of the pan and turn the cake out onto a plate, then use a cake plate to flip the cake again so it is right side up. Serve warm with Whipped Cream (page 197), plain or flavored with Kahlúa.

Orange Chocolate Cake

Chocolate and orange are natural partners, creating a great balance between acidic orange and sweet chocolate. While the glazed cake looks impressive enough, once you cut it open, you get the full visual impact. We could've made it an ordinary marble cake, but instead we floated one layer over the other: we like to call it a no-layer layer cake. The intense orange flavor in the cake comes from adding the orange zest to the hot liquid, which releases the oils in the zest and allows the flavor to infuse the liquid. The glaze is simple, a translucent sheen of chocolate speckled with slightly bitter pieces of orange rind. Though the glaze is very sweet, when combined with the cake, it rounds out and complements the other flavors. **Serves 8 to 10**

Baking spray with flour or unsalted butter and
*   all-purpose flour for the pan*

1 Basic Cake Recipe (page 12)

1 tablespoon grated orange zest

¼ cup fresh orange juice (from 1 orange)

3 ounces semisweet chocolate, chopped

For the glaze

1 cup orange marmalade

2 ounces semisweet chocolate, chopped

Preheat the oven to 350°F and position a rack in the center. Grease and flour a 9-inch round cake pan.

Prepare the cake batter according to the recipe, with the following changes: In Step 2, add the orange zest to the warm milk and butter, and add the orange juice with the vanilla. In Step 5, melt the chocolate in a large bowl in the microwave, or melt the chocolate in a double boiler and then transfer it to a large bowl (this must be done at the last minute so the chocolate doesn't set). Add half the cake batter to the chocolate and stir quickly but gently until they are completely combined and no streaks remain.

Pour the chocolate batter into the prepared pan. Hold a rubber spatula parallel to the surface of the cake and slowly pour the plain batter over the spatula and onto the chocolate batter.

Bake for 30 to 40 minutes, until the edges pull back from the pan and a toothpick inserted in the center of the cake comes out clean. Set the cake on a rack to cool.

When the cake is cool, run a knife around the edge of the pan and turn the cake out onto a plate, then use a cake plate to flip the cake again so it is right side up.

Prepare the glaze: Combine the marmalade and chocolate in a small saucepan set over medium heat. Cook, stirring often, until the chocolate is melted and the glaze begins to simmer at the edges, about 5 minutes. Let sit off the heat for 5 minutes to cool slightly.

Pour the warm glaze onto the center of the cake. Using an offset spatula, spread the glaze evenly over the top of the cake and the sides; the glaze should drip down the sides. Let stand until the glaze is set and no longer tacky, about 30 minutes, before serving.

Orange Cranberry Walnut Cake

Who says cranberries only belong on the Thanksgiving table? Chewy dried cranberries are great any time of year, but especially in this cake, with the complementary flavors of orange and walnut. We don't toast the walnuts; toasting tends to bring out their bitterness. Be sure to grind the cranberries very fine; if they are too big, they will clump and sink to the bottom of the cake.

Serve this cake for breakfast or brunch, or set it out with coffee and tea when guests come calling during the Christmas season. We prefer it plain, but you can gild the lily and serve it with Vanilla Ice Cream (page 184). **Serves 8 to 10**

Baking spray or butter for the pan

⅔ cup (about 4 ounces) walnuts

1 Basic Cake Recipe (page 12)

1 cup dried cranberries

1½ teaspoons grated orange zest

Preheat the oven to 350°F and position a rack in the center. Generously grease a 9-inch round cake pan.

Pulse the walnuts in a food processor until the bulk of the nuts are the size of small peas (there will also be some walnut dust). Pour the walnuts into the bottom of the prepared pan and shake to distribute them evenly.

Prepare the batter according to the recipe, with the following changes: In Step 1, place the cranberries in the food processor bowl (don't bother to wash the bowl; the walnut residue will flavor the cake) and process until very finely ground, about 30 seconds. Add the flour and baking powder and pulse to combine; the mixture will resemble coarse sand. In Step 2, add the orange zest to the warm milk and butter mixture.

Pour the batter into the prepared pan. Bake for 30 to 40 minutes, until the edges pull back from the pan and a toothpick inserted in the center of the cake comes out clean. Set the cake on a rack to cool for 10 minutes.

Run a knife around the edge of the pan and turn the cake out onto a cake plate. Serve warm or at room temperature. (Do not refrigerate; the nuts will get soggy.)

Pineapple Macadamia Nut Cake

Here's a Hawaiian-inspired cake that's just the thing for a barbecue or picnic, because it travels well. The pineapple adds incredible moistness to the cake, and the macadamia nuts create a crunchy topping. **Serves 8 to 10**

Baking spray or butter for the pan

1 cup (about 4 ounces) macadamia nuts, ground

⅔ cup canned crushed pineapple (from a 20-ounce can)

1 Basic Cake Recipe (page 12), minus the vanilla

Preheat the oven to 350°F and position a rack in the center. Generously grease a 9-inch round cake pan.

Pour the macadamia nuts into the pan and shake to distribute them evenly.

Drain the pineapple thoroughly by squeezing it in small batches in your hand to remove all the juice. (Save the juice for a piña colada or drink it.)

Prepare the cake batter according to the recipe, with the following changes: In Step 2, omit the vanilla. In Step 5, gently fold the pineapple into the finished batter.

Pour the batter into the prepared pan. Bake for 30 to 40 minutes, until the edges pull back from the pan and a toothpick inserted in the center of the cake comes out clean. Set the cake on a rack to cool.

When the cake is cool, run a knife around the edge of the pan and turn the cake out onto a cake plate. Serve with Whipped Cream (page 197), plain or flavored with rum.

Plum Cognac Cake

Because prunes have gotten a bad rap, they are now being marketed as "dried plums." Whatever you call them, prunes and Cognac are a classic dessert combination. The result is a sophisticated cake that's not too sweet and is ideal for brunch. The prunes are ground with the Cognac and hot water and added to the batter, creating jammy pockets of flavor throughout the cake. **Serves 8**

Baking spray with flour or unsalted butter and
  all-purpose flour for the pan

2 cups (about 12 ounces) pitted prunes

¼ cup Cognac, Armagnac, or brandy

1 Basic Cake Recipe (page 12)

½ teaspoon ground cinnamon

Confectioners' sugar

Preheat the oven to 350°F and position a rack in the center. Grease and flour a 9-inch round cake pan.

Combine the prunes, Cognac, and ¼ cup hot water in a food processor and process until the prunes are very finely ground and the mixture is thick and jammy.

Prepare the batter according to the recipe, with the following changes: In Step 1, add the cinnamon to the flour and baking powder. In Step 5, quickly but gently fold the prune mixture into the finished batter until just combined.

Pour the batter into the prepared pan. Bake for 30 to 40 minutes, until the edges pull back from the pan and a toothpick inserted in the center of the cake comes out clean. Set the cake on a rack to cool.

When the cake is cool, run a knife around the edge of the pan and turn the cake out onto a plate, then use a cake plate to flip the cake again so it is right side up. Dust with confectioners' sugar just before serving.

Pumpkin Cake

Pumpkin pie has its place, but when we crave the flavor of pumpkin paired with autumn spices, we turn to this cake. It gets even better with age, so make it ahead—or save some for later. **Serves 8 to 10**

*Baking spray with flour or unsalted butter and
all-purpose flour for the pan*

1 cup canned pumpkin puree

1 tablespoon brandy

*1 Basic Cake Recipe (page 12), minus ¼ cup
of the granulated sugar*

½ teaspoon ground cinnamon

¼ teaspoon ground nutmeg

¼ teaspoon ground ginger

¼ cup packed dark brown sugar

*½ cup (about 3 ounces) walnuts, finely chopped,
plus extra for garnish, if desired*

Preheat oven to 350°F; position a rack in the center. Grease and flour a 9-inch round cake pan.

Combine the pumpkin and brandy in a large bowl and stir until combined.

Prepare the batter according to the recipe, with the following changes: In Step 1, add the spices to the flour and baking powder. In Step 3, replace ¼ cup of the granulated sugar with the dark brown sugar. In Step 5, add about 1 cup of batter to the pumpkin mixture and stir until combined. Add half of the remaining batter to the pumpkin and gently fold to combine. Repeat with the remaining batter. Quickly but gently fold in the walnuts until just combined.

Pour the batter into the prepared pan. Bake for 30 to 40 minutes, until the edges pull back from the pan and a toothpick inserted in the center of the cake comes out clean. Set the cake on a rack to cool for 10 minutes.

Run a knife around the edge of the pan and turn the cake out onto a plate, then use a cake plate to flip the cake again so it is right side up. Serve warm or at room temperature, with Whipped Cream (page 197) flavored with brandy. Sprinkle with chopped walnuts, if desired.

Raspberry Almond Cake

Using jam in baking was a colonial practice, since the only fruit available during the long winters was what had been preserved during the summer. Although this is a great brunch cake any time of year, we find it perfect for providing a taste of summer in the winter. Feel free to substitute strawberry, orange, or blackberry jam. **Serves 8 to 10**

Baking spray or butter for the pan

½ cup plus ⅓ cup sliced almonds

1 Basic Cake Recipe (page 12)

½ cup seedless raspberry jam

Preheat the oven to 350°F and position a rack in the center. Generously grease a 9-inch round cake pan.

Toast the almonds in a medium skillet over medium-high heat until lightly browned and aromatic, 5 to 7 minutes. Let cool.

With your hands, gently crush ⅓ cup of the almonds. Spread them over the bottom of the prepared pan.

Prepare the batter according to the recipe, with the following changes: In Step 2, add the raspberry jam to the warm milk and butter and stir to melt completely. In Step 5, fold the remaining ½ cup almonds into the finished batter.

Pour the batter into the prepared pan. Bake for 30 to 40 minutes, until the edges pull back from the pan and a toothpick inserted in the center of the cake comes out clean. Set the cake on a rack to cool for 10 minutes.

Run a knife around the edge of the pan and turn the cake out onto a cake plate. Serve warm or at room temperature.

Tiramisu Cheesecake

Tiramisu—its name translates literally as "pick me up," because of the high sugar content and the caffeine from the espresso—may be Italian in origin, but it has become a fixture on American dessert menus. Our cheesecake version is denser than typical tiramisu, but it's also much easier. Traditional tiramisu has numerous components—ladyfingers, zabaglione, syrup—that can take all day to prepare. Ours is made all in one pan and without a cooked custard, which will leave you plenty of time for your own pick-me-up—a cup of coffee with a splash of leftover Marsala.

Be careful when working with mascarpone; overmixing will cause it to break (the fat will separate) and curdle. And make sure you use hot water for the water bath—if the water bath isn't hot going into the oven, it will take longer for the cake to cook.

Like any cheesecake, this one must set overnight, or for at least 8 hours, in the refrigerator, so plan accordingly. **Serves 10 to 12**

Baking spray or butter for the pan

12 ladyfinger cookies (about 6 ounces), such as Stella D'oro Margherites (or any plain cookie), to yield 1¾ cups when ground

1 tablespoon ground coffee

4 tablespoons (½ stick) unsalted butter, melted

1 pound mascarpone

¾ cup sugar

¼ cup sweet or dry Marsala

2 tablespoons dark rum

1 cup heavy cream

1 Basic Cake Recipe (page 12)

Semisweet chocolate shavings (page 10), optional

Preheat the oven to 350°F and position a rack in the center. Grease a 9-inch springform pan. Wrap the bottom and sides of the pan in a double layer of aluminum foil to prevent leaks (even the best springform pans can leak a bit).

Grind the ladyfingers and coffee in a food processor until fine, about 30 seconds (if any large pieces of the ladyfingers remain, break them up with your fingers and then pulse a few more times). Add the butter and pulse 3 to 5 times, until the mixture resembles wet sand. Pour into the prepared pan and shake to distribute the crumbs evenly, then press them into a compact, even layer with your fingers or the bottom of a metal measuring cup.

Bake the crust for 10 minutes, or until lightly browned. Set on a rack to cool. (Leave the oven on.)

Place the mascarpone and sugar in a large bowl and stir gently just until well blended; do not overmix. Add the Marsala and rum and stir gently until combined. Whip the cream to soft peaks (see page 7) and gently fold in until just combined.

Prepare the cake batter according to the recipe. Add about 1 cup of the batter to the mascarpone mixture and stir until combined. Add half the remaining batter to the mascarpone and gently fold to combine. Repeat with the remaining batter.

Pour the batter into the prepared pan. Place the pan in a larger pan, such as a roasting pan, and fill the larger pan with hot water to come about halfway up the sides of the springform pan. Bake for 65 to 70 minutes, until all but the very center of the cake is set (the center should jiggle slightly when the pan is shaken).

Remove the cake from the oven and let it sit in the water bath for 15 minutes. Remove the cake from the water, remove the foil wrapping (be careful, as water tends to collect inside the foil), and set the cake on a rack to cool. Run a knife around the edge of the pan to release the cake, but do not remove the ring.

Allow the cake to cool, then refrigerate at least 8 hours, or overnight, until chilled and completely set. Remove from the refrigerator and let sit at room temperature for 30 minutes before removing the ring and serving.

Garnish with chocolate shavings, if desired.

Upside-Down Cakes

There's something fun about upside-down cakes. Maybe it's the element of surprise when you turn out the cake, not knowing exactly what it will look like. Maybe it's the allure of the hot topping dripping down the sides of the cake. Or maybe it's the way it starts out one way—right side up—and ends up completely different.

In this chapter, you'll find the whole gamut of upside-down cakes, from the original Tarte Tatin to the decidedly modern Burnt Sugar Cake. But in every case, the warm toppings permeate the cake, adding another layer of flavor and complexity. Because of the moist toppings, these cakes won't keep for more than 2 days, wrapped well, at room temperature.

When pouring the batter into the pan over the topping, make sure the force of the batter doesn't disrupt the layer of topping. The best way to do this is to pour slowly in a circular motion around the pan (rather than directly into the center of the pan). Pouring slowly means less pressure will be applied, and the batter will be less likely to disturb the topping.

Despite your best efforts at generously greasing the pan, there will be times when a small amount of topping sticks to the pan. Don't worry about it—just scoop the stuck part from the pan and patch it onto the cake. No one will be able to tell.

Tarte Tatin

Tarte Tatin, the original upside-down cake, was invented by the Tatin sisters, who ran a hotel in the Loire Valley of France in the late 1800s. Legends surrounding the dessert vary, but most agree that it was the result of lucky happenstance: one of the sisters (our favorite version has her distracted by a handsome fellow) accidentally prepared her famous apple tart upside down and served it warm—and the rest is history. Here we simplify things, creating the same delicious dessert with our easy-to-make cake instead of time-consuming puff pastry. Be sure to use firm apples, though, or you'll end up with applesauce cake. **Serves 10 to 12**

Baking spray or butter for the pan

For the topping

1 cup sugar

4 tablespoons (½ stick) unsalted butter, cut into 4 pieces

4 medium tart firm apples, like Granny Smith (about 2 pounds), peeled, cored, and cut into quarters

For the cake

1 Basic Cake Recipe (page 12)

Preheat the oven to 350°F and position a rack in the center. Generously grease a 10-inch round cake pan.

Combine the sugar and butter in a medium skillet, preferably nonstick, over medium-high heat. Stir constantly until the butter melts and the mixture comes to a boil (it will look granular). Continue stirring until the mixture is deep nutty brown, smooth, and shiny, 3 to 5 minutes. Lay the apples on the curved side in concentric circles in the skillet; the caramel may harden a bit at the edges of the apples. Cook over low heat until the apples begin to soften, moving the apples with a fork so that any hardened caramel is completely melted, 3 to 5 minutes. Flip all the apples and bring the caramel back to an active simmer. Cook 5 minutes longer. Pour into the prepared pan and tilt the pan to coat the bottom evenly with caramel. Working quickly, using tongs or two forks, again arrange the apples in concentric circles (see illustration).

Prepare the cake batter according to the recipe.

Pour the batter evenly over the apples. Bake for 30 to 40 minutes, until the edges pull back from the pan and a toothpick inserted in the center of the cake comes out clean.

Let the cake sit on a rack to set for 5 minutes.

Run a knife around the edge of the pan to loosen the cake, place a plate over the pan, and carefully flip the cake onto the plate (be sure to use pot holders or a kitchen towel, as the pan will be extremely hot).

Serve warm with Vanilla Ice Cream (page 184).

Crumb Upside-Down Cake

Many of us remember Drake's coffee cakes from our youth, those compact little snacks with the sweet crumb topping. This is our version, and far better, we might add. It's the ultimate brunch cake, simple and basic, needing only a cup of strong coffee to go with it. Be prepared for folks to come running when you bake this: as the crumb topping bakes, the rich smells of vanilla and cinnamon fill the air. **Serves 8 to 10**

Baking spray with flour or unsalted butter and
*   all-purpose flour for the pan*

For the topping

1 cup all-purpose flour

¾ cup sugar

¼ teaspoon salt

½ teaspoon ground cinnamon

1 teaspoon vanilla extract

8 tablespoons (1 stick) cold unsalted butter, cut into 8 pieces

For the cake

1 Basic Cake Recipe (page 12)

Preheat the oven to 350°F and position a rack in the center. Grease and flour a 10-inch round cake pan.

Process the flour, sugar, salt, cinnamon, and vanilla in a food processor until combined, about 5 seconds. Add the butter and process until the mixture begins to clump together, about 20 seconds. Spread the mixture in an even layer in the prepared pan, breaking up any large clumps.

Prepare the cake batter according to the recipe.

Pour the batter evenly over the crumb topping. Bake for 30 to 40 minutes, until the edges pull back from the pan and a toothpick inserted in the center of the cake comes out clean. Let the cake sit on a rack to set for 5 minutes.

Run a knife around the edge of the pan to loosen the cake, place a plate over the pan, and carefully flip the cake onto the plate (be sure to use pot holders or a kitchen towel, as the pan will be extremely hot).

Serve warm or at room temperature.

Bananas Foster Upside-Down Cake

Bananas Foster was created at Brennan's restaurant in New Orleans in 1951, the result of a challenge from owner Owen Edward Brennan to his chef to come up with a dish using the plentiful bananas that entered the U.S. through the New Orleans port. The dish was named for Richard Foster, chairman of the New Orleans Crime Commission. The traditional version is prepared tableside and flambéed, but our version takes the best of the dish and pairs it with cake. Make sure your bananas are ripe: underripe bananas will lack taste, and overripe bananas will turn to mush. **Serves 10 to 12**

Baking spray or butter for the pan

For the topping

¼ cup dark rum

4 tablespoons (½ stick) unsalted butter, cut into 4 pieces

¾ cup packed dark brown sugar

4 ripe but not soft medium bananas, sliced into ¼-inch disks

For the cake

1 Basic Cake Recipe (page 12)

Preheat the oven to 350°F and position a rack in the center. Generously grease a 10-inch round cake pan.

Combine the rum, butter, and brown sugar in a medium skillet over medium-high heat. Stir constantly until the butter melts and the mixture is smooth. Bring to a boil, stirring occasionally. When the surface bubbles and foams, remove from the heat. Add the bananas and toss gently to combine. Pour into the prepared pan and spread in an even layer.

Prepare the cake batter according to the recipe. Pour the batter evenly over the banana mixture. Bake for 30 to 40 minutes, until the edges pull back from the pan and a toothpick inserted in the center of the cake comes out clean. Let the cake sit on a rack to set for 5 minutes.

Run a knife around the edge of the pan to loosen the cake, place a plate over the pan, and carefully flip the cake onto the plate (be sure to use pot holders or a kitchen towel, as the pan will be extremely hot). Serve warm with Vanilla Ice Cream (page 184).

Burnt Sugar Upside-Down Cake

This is topped with the thin crème brûlée coating of crisp caramel that shatters like glass when tapped with the edge of your fork. Instead of creamy custard beneath, however, you'll find tender, moist cake.

Make sure the toffee pieces are dry and still crunchy (toffee sometimes gets soft when it is old or the air is very humid); if they are soft, the ground toffee will sink into the cake. And when making the burnt sugar topping, be sure to have a thin, even layer of sugar in the pan—if the sugar is piled up unevenly, the bottom will burn before the top layer melts. **Serves 10 to 12**

Baking spray or butter for the pan

For the topping

¾ cup sugar

For the cake

1 Basic Cake Recipe (page 12), minus ½ cup of the sugar

½ cup toffee pieces (like Heath Bar bits), finely ground

½ cup packed dark brown sugar

Preheat the oven to 350°F and position a rack in the center. Generously grease a 10-inch round cake pan.

Spread the sugar in an even layer in a dry 12-inch stainless steel skillet over high heat. Cook the sugar, without stirring, until about two-thirds of it has melted and turned a light amber color, 3 to 5 minutes. Stir to combine—the stirring will cause the remaining sugar to melt. Remove from the heat and pour into the prepared pan. Tilt the pan to coat the bottom evenly—work quickly, as the caramel will begin to set. And be careful—the cake pan will become very hot!

Prepare the cake batter according to the recipe, with the following changes: In Step 1, add the ground toffee to the flour mixture. In Step 3, replace ½ cup of the granulated sugar with the dark brown sugar.

Pour the batter evenly over the sugar mixture. Bake for 30 to 40 minutes until the edges pull back from the pan and a toothpick inserted in the center of the cake comes out clean. Let the cake sit on a rack to set for 5 minutes.

Run a knife around the edge of the pan to loosen the cake, place a plate over the pan, and carefully flip the cake onto the plate (be sure to use pot holders or a kitchen towel, as the pan will be extremely hot). Let cool.

Serve at room temperature. (Do not refrigerate this cake—refrigeration will cause the burnt sugar layer to turn soft and wet.)

Chocolate Cherry Caramel Upside-Down Cake

Who doesn't love chocolate-covered cherries? Now imagine them dipped in caramel and served warm and delightfully gooey, and you'll have a good idea of what this cake tastes like. Be sure to use sweet, not sour, cherries. **Serves 10 to 12**

Baking spray or butter for the pan

For the topping

1 cup sugar

4 tablespoons (½ stick) unsalted butter, cut into 4 pieces

½ cup heavy cream

1½ pounds frozen sweet cherries, thawed, drained,
    and squeezed to remove excess juice

For the cake

1 Basic Cake Recipe (page 12)

3 tablespoons kirsch or other cherry-flavored liqueur

8 ounces semisweet chocolate, chopped

Preheat the oven to 350°F and position a rack in the center. Generously grease a 10-inch round cake pan.

Combine the sugar, butter, and cream in a large skillet over medium-high heat. Stir constantly until the butter melts and the mixture is smooth, then stir occasionally until the mixture begins to turn a golden toffee color, 4 to 5 minutes. Stir vigorously to combine, and add the cherries; the mixture will sizzle and seize. Stir to combine, breaking up any lumps of caramel with the edge of the spoon. Continue to cook, stirring occasionally, until the mixture is smooth and thick, about 10 minutes. Pour the mixture into the prepared pan and tilt to coat the bottom of the pan evenly.

While the cherry caramel is cooking, prepare the cake batter according to the recipe, with the following changes: In Step 2, add the kirsch with the vanilla. In Step 5, melt the chocolate in a large bowl in the microwave, or melt the chocolate in a double boiler and then transfer it to a large bowl (this must be done at the last minute so the chocolate doesn't set). Add the warm milk and butter to the chocolate and stir until combined, then add the chocolate to half of the batter. Stir quickly but gently until the chocolate is evenly distributed. Gently fold the chocolate batter into the remaining batter until completely combined and no streaks remain.

Pour the batter evenly over the cherry mixture. Bake for 30 to 40 minutes, until the edges pull back from the pan and a toothpick inserted in the center of the cake comes out with a few moist crumbs but is not wet. Let the cake sit on a rack to set for 5 minutes.

Run a knife around the edge of the pan to loosen the cake, place a plate over the pan, and carefully flip the cake onto the plate (be sure to use pot holders or a kitchen towel, as the pan will be extremely hot).

Serve warm with Whipped Cream (page 197), plain or flavored with kirsch.

Chocolate Peanut Butter Upside-Down Cake

Though we can't take credit for inventing this combination, we can say we've perfected it in cake form. It's great for kids, and though they might be tempted to eat it right out of the pan, it's actually better at room temperature. Can't get enough chocolate and peanut butter? Be sure to try the Peanut Butter Cup Cakes (page 100). **Serves 10 to 12**

Baking spray or butter for the pan

For the topping

1 cup sugar

2 tablespoons corn syrup

1¼ cups milk

4 tablespoons (½ stick) unsalted butter, cut into 4 pieces

Pinch of salt

⅔ cup crunchy peanut butter

For the cake

1 Basic Cake Recipe (page 12)

8 ounces semisweet chocolate, chopped

Preheat the oven to 350°F and position a rack in the center. Generously grease a 10-inch round cake pan.

Combine the sugar, corn syrup, milk, butter, and salt in a medium saucepan over medium-high heat. Stir constantly until the butter melts and the mixture comes to a boil. Continue to cook, stirring occasionally, until the mixture begins to turn a light golden color, 8 to 10 minutes. Remove from the heat.

Add the peanut butter and stir vigorously to combine; the mixture should be smooth and shiny. Pour into the prepared pan and tilt to coat the bottom of the pan evenly.

Prepare the cake batter according to the recipe, with the following change: In Step 5, melt the chocolate in a large bowl in the microwave, or melt the chocolate in a double boiler and then transfer it to a large bowl (this must be done at the last minute so the chocolate doesn't set). Add the warm milk and butter to the chocolate and stir until combined, then add the chocolate to half of the batter. Stir quickly but gently until the chocolate is evenly distributed. Gently fold the chocolate batter into the remaining batter until completely combined and no streaks remain.

Pour the batter evenly over the peanut butter mixture. Bake for 30 to 40 minutes, until the edges pull back from the pan and a toothpick inserted in the center of the cake comes out clean. Let the cake sit on a rack to set for 5 minutes.

Run a knife around the edge of the pan to loosen the cake, place a plate over the pan, and carefully flip the cake onto the plate (be sure to use pot holders or a kitchen towel, as the pan will be extremely hot). Let cool to room temperature before serving.

Dulce de Leche Upside-Down Cake

Literally "milk candy" or "milk jam," the Latin confection called *dulce de leche* is so easy to make . . . all you do is cook sweetened condensed milk. Its flavor is unique: a sweet, creamy caramel custard. The neatest thing about this cake is its complete transformation: you pour in a simple can of sweetened condensed milk and turn out a cake with a sweet caramel topping. **Serves 10 to 12**

Baking spray or butter for the pan

For the topping
One 14-ounce can sweetened condensed milk

For the cake
1 Basic Cake Recipe (page 12)

¼ cup Kahlúa

Preheat the oven to 350°F and position a rack in the center. Generously grease a 10-inch round cake pan.

Pour the condensed milk into the prepared pan and tilt to spread it evenly.

Prepare the cake batter according to the recipe, with the following change: In Step 2, add the Kahlúa with the vanilla.

Pour the batter evenly over the condensed milk. Bake for 30 to 40 minutes, until the edges pull back from the pan and a toothpick inserted in the center of the cake comes out clean. Let the cake sit on a rack to set for 5 minutes.

Run a knife around the edge of the pan to loosen the cake, place a plate over the pan, and carefully flip the cake onto the plate (be sure to use pot holders or a kitchen towel, as the pan will be extremely hot).

Serve warm or at room temperature.

Honey Nut Upside-Down Cake

This is a great dinner party cake because it's a real showstopper, yet incredibly easy to make. We love the sweet and salty combination (be sure to use salted nuts) and the caramel quality of the honey. Don't be tempted to serve the cake warm; the nuts will be soft rather than crunchy. **Serves 10 to 12**

Baking spray or butter for the pan

For the topping

1 cup honey

2 tablespoons unsalted butter

*One 10-ounce can (about 2 cups) mixed salted nuts
   (we prefer the "deluxe" version, without peanuts)*

For the cake

1 Basic Cake Recipe (page 12)

Preheat the oven to 350°F and position a rack in the center. Generously grease a 10-inch round cake pan.

Bring the honey and butter to a boil in a small saucepan over medium-high heat. Add the nuts and stir to combine. Reduce the heat to medium and cook until the honey is thickened and deep golden brown, 6 to 8 minutes. Pour into the prepared pan and tilt to spread in an even layer.

Prepare the cake batter according to the recipe.

Pour the batter evenly over the nut mixture. Bake for 30 to 40 minutes, until the edges pull back from the pan and a toothpick inserted in the center of the cake comes out clean. Let the cake sit on a rack to set for 5 minutes.

Run a knife around the edge of the pan to loosen the cake, place a plate over the pan, and carefully flip the cake onto the plate (be sure to use pot holders or a kitchen towel, as the pan will be extremely hot). Let cool to room temperature before serving.

Hot Fudge Upside-Down Cake

To us, hot fudge is a reward, a special treat. The simplicity of this cake is what makes it so versatile. It's good with whipped cream, better with ice cream, and just perfect with both, topped with a sweet cherry. It's also good topped with sliced bananas or chocolate sprinkles. And even though it is a hot fudge cake, it's good cold or at room temperature—when it's thick, moist, and fudgy. **Serves 10 to 12**

Baking spray or butter for the pan

For the topping
1 recipe Hot Fudge Sauce (page 195)

For the cake
1 Basic Cake Recipe (page 12)

¼ cup cocoa powder, whisked to remove lumps

Preheat the oven to 350°F and position a rack in the center. Generously grease a 10-inch round cake pan.

Prepare the hot fudge. Pour into the prepared pan and spread in an even layer.

Prepare the cake batter according to the recipe, with the following change: In Step 1, add the cocoa to the flour mixture.

Pour the batter evenly over the hot fudge. Bake for 30 to 40 minutes, or until the edges pull back from the pan and a toothpick inserted in the center of the cake comes out clean. Let the cake sit on a rack to set for 5 minutes.

Run a knife around the edge of the pan to loosen the cake, place a plate over the pan, and carefully flip the cake onto the plate (be sure to use pot holders or a kitchen towel, as the pan will be extremely hot).

Serve immediately with Vanilla Ice Cream (page 184), at room temperature with a cold glass of milk, or chilled.

Maple Cranberry Upside-Down Cake

In New England, where we live, maple and cranberry are two quintessentially autumn ingredients. They find their way into everything from pancakes to bread, stuffing to squash. So why not cake? Serve at Thanksgiving, instead of (or along with) the pumpkin pie. **Serves 10 to 12**

Baking spray or butter for the pan

For the topping

1 cup maple syrup, preferably grade B

8 ounces (2 cups) frozen cranberries, thawed

For the cake

*1 Basic Cake Recipe (page 12), minus ¼ cup
    of the granulated sugar*

¼ cup packed dark brown sugar

Preheat the oven to 350°F and position a rack in the center. Generously grease a 10-inch round cake pan.

Bring the maple syrup to a boil in a medium saucepan over medium-high heat. Reduce the heat to medium and cook until the syrup is reduced by half, 5 to 7 minutes (be careful, as the mixture may boil over). Remove from the heat and add the cranberries, stirring to coat evenly. Pour into the prepared pan and spread in an even layer.

Prepare the cake batter according to the recipe, with the following change: In Step 3, replace ¼ cup of the granulated sugar with the dark brown sugar.

Pour the batter evenly into the pan. Bake for 30 to 40 minutes, or until the edges pull back from the pan and a toothpick inserted in the center of the cake comes out clean. Let the cake sit on a rack to set for 5 minutes.

Run a knife around the edge of the pan to loosen the cake, place a plate over the pan, and carefully flip the cake onto the plate (be sure to use pot holders or a kitchen towel, as the pan will be extremely hot).

Serve warm or at room temperature.

Mocha Pecan Upside-Down Cake

Greg has long been a fan of the mocha–pecan combination. There's something very autumnal about the earthy flavors of coffee and pecans. Of course chocolate is good all year round. Coffee and chocolate go together so well because the underlying bitterness of the coffee rounds out the sweet richness of the chocolate. **Serves 10 to 12**

Baking spray or butter for the pan

For the topping

1 tablespoon instant coffee

½ cup hot coffee

½ cup heavy cream

1½ cups pecan halves

2 cups confectioners' sugar

For the cake

1 Basic Cake Recipe (page 12)

1 cup finely ground pecans

4 ounces semisweet chocolate, chopped

Preheat the oven to 350°F and position a rack in the center. Generously grease a 10-inch round cake pan.

Stir the instant coffee into the brewed coffee until completely dissolved, then add the heavy cream. Set aside.

Combine the pecans and sugar in a medium skillet over medium-high heat. Stir constantly until the sugar is completely melted; the mixture will turn a deep toffee color. Add the coffee mixture, holding your hand away from the pan—the mixture will bubble and seize. Reduce the heat to low, cover the pan, and cook for 2 minutes. Uncover the pan and stir until the caramel is smooth, about 1 minute longer. Pour into the prepared pan and spread in an even layer.

Prepare the cake batter according to the recipe, with the following changes: In Step 1, add the ground pecans to the flour mixture. In Step 5, melt the chocolate in a large bowl in the microwave, or melt the chocolate in a double boiler and then transfer it to a large bowl (this must be done at the last minute so the chocolate doesn't set). Add the warm milk and butter to the chocolate and stir until combined, then add the chocolate to half of the batter. Stir quickly but gently until the chocolate is evenly distributed. Gently fold the chocolate batter into the remaining batter until completely combined and no streaks remain.

Pour the batter evenly over the pecans. Bake for 30 to 40 minutes, or until the edges pull back from the pan and a toothpick inserted in the center of the cake comes out with a few moist crumbs but is not wet. Let the cake sit on a rack to set for 5 minutes.

Run a knife around the edge of the pan to loosen the cake, place a plate over the pan, and carefully flip the cake onto the plate (be sure to use pot holders or a kitchen towel, as the pan will be extremely hot). Serve warm.

Oatmeal Apricot Upside-Down Cake

Because dried apricots vary greatly in sweetness, taste yours first, and use the lesser amount of sugar if the apricots are sweet. **Serves 10 to 12**

*Baking spray with flour or unsalted butter and
all-purpose flour for the pan*

For the topping

6 ounces dried apricots, chopped (about 1 cup)

⅔ to ¾ cup sugar (see headnote)

For the cake

*1 Basic Cake Recipe (page 12), minus ½ cup
of the granulated sugar*

¾ cup old-fashioned oats (not quick or instant)

½ teaspoon ground cinnamon

½ cup packed dark brown sugar

Preheat oven to 350°F; position a rack in the center. Grease and flour a 10-inch round cake pan.

Combine the apricots, sugar, and 2 cups water in a small saucepan over medium-high heat. Bring to a boil and cook until the apricots begin to break down and the mixture is thickened and syrupy, 6 to 8 minutes. Gently mash the apricots with a potato masher so the mixture is jamlike. Pour into the prepared pan and tilt to spread in an even layer.

Prepare cake batter according to the recipe, with these changes: In Step 1, add oats and cinnamon to flour mixture. In Step 2, replace ½ cup of the granulated sugar with dark brown sugar.

Pour the batter evenly over the apricots. Bake for 30 to 40 minutes, or until the edges pull back from the pan and a toothpick inserted in the center of the cake comes out clean. Let the cake sit on a rack to set for 5 minutes.

Run a knife around the edge of the pan to loosen the cake, place a plate over the pan, and carefully flip the cake onto the plate (be sure to use pot holders or a kitchen towel, as the pan will be extremely hot). Let cool to room temperature before serving.

Orange Grand Marnier Upside-Down Cake

We love the restrained elegance of this cake and the complex sweet and bitter flavor of the marmalade. It's simple and striking, perfect for a festive brunch. **Serves 10 to 12**

Baking spray or butter for the pan

For the topping
One 18-ounce jar orange marmalade

For the cake
1 Basic Cake Recipe (page 12)

¼ cup Grand Marnier or other orange-flavored liqueur

Preheat the oven to 350°F and position a rack in the center. Generously grease a 10-inch round cake pan.

Melt the orange marmalade in a small saucepan over medium heat. Pour into the prepared pan and tilt to spread in an even layer.

Prepare the cake batter according to the recipe, with the following change: In Step 2, add the Grand Marnier with the vanilla.

Pour the batter evenly over the marmalade. Bake for 30 to 40 minutes, or until the edges pull back from the pan and a toothpick inserted in the center of the cake comes out clean. Let the cake sit on a rack to set for 5 minutes.

Run a knife around the edge of the pan to loosen the cake, place a plate over the pan, and carefully flip the cake onto the plate (be sure to use pot holders or a kitchen towel, as the pan will be extremely hot).

Serve warm or at room temperature.

Peach Ginger Upside-Down Cake

This cake gets its ginger punch from two types of ginger—candied ginger in the topping and powdered ginger in the cake. The ground spice has a mellow flavor that completely permeates the cake, while the candied ginger bits in the topping give tiny bursts of extra flavor. Though we find frozen peaches easier to use, especially in the off-season, feel free to use fresh: use 3 large peaches (about 1½ pounds), peeled, pitted, and each cut into eighths. **Serves 10 to 12**

Baking spray or butter for the pan

For the topping

¾ cup sugar

4 tablespoons (½ stick) unsalted butter

¼ cup heavy cream

2 tablespoons finely chopped crystallized ginger

One 16-ounce bag frozen sliced peaches, thawed

For the cake

1 Basic Cake Recipe (page 12)

½ teaspoon ground ginger

Preheat the oven to 350°F and position a rack in the center. Generously grease a 10-inch round cake pan.

Combine the sugar, butter, and heavy cream in a medium skillet over medium-high heat. Stir constantly until the butter melts and the mixture is smooth, then stir occasionally until the mixture begins to turn golden brown, 6 to 8 minutes. Remove from the heat, add the crystallized ginger, and stir vigorously to combine.

Pour the caramel mixture into the prepared pan and tilt the pan to coat the bottom evenly. Arrange the peaches atop the caramel in concentric circles.

Prepare the cake batter according to the recipe, with the following change: In Step 1, add the ground ginger to the flour mixture.

Pour the batter evenly over the peaches. Bake for 30 to 40 minutes, or until the edges pull back from the pan and a toothpick inserted in the center of the cake comes out clean. Let the cake sit on a rack to set for 5 minutes.

Run a knife around the edge of the pan to loosen the cake, place a plate over the pan, and carefully flip the cake onto the plate (be sure to use pot holders or a kitchen towel, as the pan will be extremely hot).

Serve warm or at room temperature.

Peanut Butter and Jelly Upside-Down Cake

This may sound like an odd idea for a cake—good in a sandwich, but in a cake? Yet we have found that almost all the sweet flavors we love can be made into a cake (or we'll die trying). No one knows exactly when the peanut butter and jelly sandwich was created, but it is widely believed that American soldiers in World War II, who were given both peanut butter and jelly in their rations, may have been involved in its creation. We know, either you love PB&J or you don't. If you're in the former camp, you'll love this very peanut buttery cake. **Serves 10 to 12**

Baking spray or butter for the pan

For the topping
One 18-ounce jar of your favorite jam
or preserves (we like strawberry)

For the cake
1 Basic Cake Recipe (page 12)

½ cup creamy peanut butter

Preheat the oven to 350°F and position a rack in the center. Generously grease a 10-inch round cake pan.

Melt the jam in a small saucepan over medium heat. Pour into the prepared pan and tilt to spread in an even layer.

Prepare the cake batter according to the recipe, with the following change: In Step 2, add the peanut butter to the hot milk and butter and stir until melted and combined.

Pour the batter evenly over the jam. Bake for 30 to 40 minutes, or until the edges pull back from the pan and a toothpick inserted in the center of the cake comes out clean. Let the cake sit on a rack to set for 5 minutes.

Run a knife around the edge of the pan to loosen the cake, place a plate over the pan, and carefully flip the cake onto the plate (be sure to use pot holders or a kitchen towel, as the pan will be extremely hot). Let cool to room temperature before serving.

Pineapple Upside-Down Cake

This classic slice of Americana dates back to the early 1900s, when canned pineapple was produced by Jim Dole. Then, in 1925, the Hawaiian Pineapple Company (now Dole Pineapple) held a recipe contest, and of the sixty thousand recipes sent in, twenty-five hundred were for pineapple upside-down cake. Clearly the cake had spread like wildfire in the years since canned pineapple was first introduced. Coincidentally, another American classic was popularized during this time, the maraschino cherry, which is no doubt why the dessert and the cherries are so inextricably linked. While we don't want to mess too much with a classic, we just can't bear to use cloyingly artificial maraschino cherries. Our version still calls for canned pineapple rings (which are much more convenient and more consistently reliable than fresh), but we use dried cherries to add a bit of color and texture. **Serves 10 to 12**

Baking spray or butter for the pan

For the topping

4 tablespoons (½ stick) unsalted butter

¾ cup packed dark brown sugar

14 pineapple rings (from two 20-ounce cans)

32 dried cherries (about ⅓ cup)

1 Basic Cake Recipe (page 12)

Preheat the oven to 350°F and position a rack in the center. Generously grease a 10-inch round cake pan.

Melt the butter with the brown sugar in a small saucepan over medium-high heat, stirring occasionally until just combined. Pour into the prepared pan and tilt the pan to coat the bottom evenly.

Cut 6 of the pineapple rings in half and arrange them side by side, cut side up, around the sides of the pan. Lay the remaining 8 rings in the bottom of the pan so that the whole bottom is covered (you may have to squeeze the rings a bit, but do not cut them). Place 4 dried cherries in the center of each ring.

Prepare the cake batter according to the recipe.

Pour the batter evenly over the pineapple. Bake for 30 to 40 minutes, or until the edges pull back from the pan and a toothpick inserted in the center of the cake comes out clean. Let the cake sit on a rack to set for 5 minutes.

Run a knife around the edge of the pan to loosen the cake, place a plate over the pan, and carefully flip the cake onto the plate (be sure to use pot holders or a kitchen towel, as the pan will be extremely hot).

Serve warm or at room temperature.

Poached Pear Upside-Down Cake

During the long, cold winter months, there's not much fresh fruit to choose from, so thank goodness for pears. Warm winter spices permeate the poached pears, giving them a rich and complex flavor that pairs perfectly with the sweet vanilla flavor of the cake. **Serves 10 to 12**

Baking spray or butter for the pan

For the topping

⅛ teaspoon ground allspice

⅛ teaspoon ground cloves

¼ teaspoon ground cinnamon

3 tablespoons brandy

½ cup sugar

4 medium firm pears (such as d'Anjou, Bartlett, or Bosc),
*   peeled, cored, and each cut into sixths*

For the cake

1 Basic Cake Recipe (page 12)

Preheat the oven to 350°F and position a rack in the center. Generously grease a 10-inch round cake pan.

Combine the spices, brandy, sugar, and 1 cup water in a large skillet over high heat and bring to a boil, stirring occasionally to dissolve the sugar. Reduce the heat to medium-high and add the pears in a single layer. Cover and cook for 5 minutes. Remove the lid and cook until the pears are soft and just beginning to brown, 10 minutes longer.

Pour the pears and their liquid into the prepared pan and arrange the pears in an even layer. If you are so inclined, you can arrange the pears in a pretty pattern (like the spokes of a wheel), but it's not necessary; if you do, be careful, as the pears will be quite hot.

Prepare the cake batter according to the recipe.

Pour the batter evenly over the pears. Bake for 30 to 40 minutes, or until the edges pull back from the pan and a toothpick inserted in the center of the cake comes out clean. Let the cake sit on a rack to set for 5 minutes.

Run a knife around the edge of the pan to loosen the cake, place a plate over the pan, and carefully flip the cake onto the plate (be sure to use pot holders or a kitchen towel, as the pan will be extremely hot).

Serve warm or at room temperature.

Strawberry Rhubarb Upside-Down Cake

These two spring ingredients go so well together because the tart rhubarb needs the sweetness of the strawberries to balance its flavor. Greg's Grandma Violet was always making rhubarb pies, since it was the only way the kids would eat the bumper crop that came up on her farm each year. **Serves 10 to 12**

Baking spray or butter and flour for the pan

For the topping

1 cup strawberry preserves

8 ounces rhubarb, trimmed and sliced ¼ inch thick

For the cake

1 Basic Cake Recipe (page 12)

½ teaspoon ground cinnamon

Preheat the oven to 350°F and position a rack in the center. Generously grease a 10-inch round cake pan.

Melt the preserves in a small saucepan over medium heat. Add the rhubarb and stir to combine. Pour into the prepared pan and tilt to spread in an even layer.

Prepare the cake batter according to the recipe, with the following change: In Step 1, add the cinnamon to the flour mixture.

Pour the batter evenly over the rhubarb mixture. Bake for 30 to 40 minutes, or until the edges pull back from the pan and a toothpick inserted in the center of the cake comes out clean. Let the cake sit on a rack to set for 5 minutes.

Run a knife around the edge of the pan to loosen the cake, place a plate over the pan, and carefully flip the cake onto the plate (be sure to use pot holders or a kitchen towel, as the pan will be extremely hot).

Serve warm or at room temperature.

Turtle Upside-Down Cake

Our take on the traditional candy is a bit more sophisticated than the turtles found in candy stores. Though this cake doesn't look like a turtle (the candies are named because they resemble turtles, with a caramel "shell" and pecan "feet"), it has the taste and texture of one. The caramel-nut topping is sinfully chewy and gooey, and the chocolate cake is satisfyingly rich and dense. This cake is perfect for kids and grown-ups alike. **Serves 10 to 12**

Baking spray or butter for the pan

For the topping
1½ cups (about 6 ounces) pecan halves

1 recipe Caramel Glaze (page 193)

For the cake
1 Basic Cake Recipe (page 12)

8 ounces semisweet chocolate, chopped

Preheat the oven to 350°F and position a rack in the center. Generously grease a 10-inch round cake pan.

Toast the pecans in a medium skillet over medium-high heat until brown and aromatic, 6 to 8 minutes. Let cool.

Prepare the caramel glaze. Pour it into the prepared pan and spread it in an even layer. Scatter the pecans over the caramel.

Prepare the cake batter according to the recipe, with the following change: In Step 5, melt the chocolate in a large bowl in the microwave, or melt the chocolate in a double boiler and then transfer it to a large bowl (this must be done at the last minute so the chocolate doesn't set). Add the warm milk and butter to the chocolate and stir until combined, then add the chocolate to half of the batter. Stir quickly but gently until the chocolate is evenly distributed. Gently fold the chocolate batter into the remaining batter until completely combined and no streaks remain.

Pour the batter evenly over the pecans. Bake for 30 to 35 minutes, or until the edges pull back from the pan and a toothpick inserted in the center of the cake comes out clean. Let the cake sit on a rack to set for 5 minutes.

Run a knife around the edge of the pan to loosen the cake, place a plate over the pan, and carefully flip the cake onto the plate (be sure to use pot holders or a kitchen towel, as the pan will be extremely hot).

Serve warm but not hot. As the cake cools, the caramel will become chewier and a little harder to slice.

Bars, Cupcakes, and Small Bites

This is the fun chapter, full of festive cupcakes, bars, and small treats that kids will love. And we were able to turn so many of our childhood favorites into cakes: Peanut Butter Cup Cakes, Milky Way Cupcakes, S'Mores Bars. But there's also an element of elegance in the plated desserts, individual delights like Mimosa Parfaits and Molten Chocolate Cakes that are sure to impress.

The desserts in this chapter are among the most visually different. Here is where you will surely find yourself repeating (as we often did), "I can't believe these all came from the same cake recipe."

Because of the large role incorporated air plays in this cake, the amount of batter you end up with may vary slightly, depending on how you beat or fold the batter. It's nothing to worry about, and in most cases you wouldn't even notice it, but it may affect the number of cupcakes you end up with; we have given an average yield for those recipes.

Amaretti Tartufi

These ice cream truffles—just ice cream, cake, and chocolate—are the perfect dinner party dessert, self-contained and beautiful. The best part is that you can prepare them days ahead of time (they will keep, tightly covered, in the freezer for a week) and then pull them out to impress your guests.

To crush the cookies, place them in a zipper-lock bag and smash them with a rolling pin or skillet. To soften the ice cream, place it in a bowl and gently break it up with a spoon until it is pliable. **Makes 12 tartufi**

For the cake

Baking spray with flour or unsalted butter and all-purpose flour for the pan

1 Basic Cake Recipe (page 12)

One 5½-ounce package Stella D'oro almond biscotti, crushed into pea-sized pieces (about 1½ cups crumbs/pieces)

For the filling and topping

1 recipe Vanilla Ice Cream (page 184) or ½ gallon store-bought vanilla ice cream, softened

1 recipe Chocolate Glaze (page 194)

Preheat the oven to 350°F and position a rack in the center. Lightly grease the bottom of an 11 by 17-inch jelly-roll pan, line it with parchment paper or aluminum foil, and grease and flour the paper.

Prepare the cake batter according to the recipe. Fold ¾ cup of the biscotti pieces into the finished batter.

Pour the batter into the prepared pan, taking care to spread it into all corners of the pan with a rubber spatula. Bake for 15 to 20 minutes, until the surface springs back when pressed with your finger and a toothpick inserted in the center of the cake comes out clean. Set the cake on a rack to cool.

When the cake is cool, run a knife around the edge of the pan and turn the cake out onto a large cutting board. Remove the parchment paper or foil. Cut out 12 rounds of cake with a

3-inch biscuit cutter. The scraps are a cook's treat. Arrange the rounds on a rack set over a baking sheet.

Combine the ice cream and the remaining biscotti pieces in a bowl. Place the ice cream in the freezer for 10 to 15 minutes to firm up (it needs to be firm enough to hold its shape when scooped).

Prepare the chocolate glaze.

Using a $\frac{1}{3}$-cup scoop, place a scoop of ice cream on each cake round. Pour the glaze over the ice cream, spreading it with an offset spatula so that all of the ice cream and cake is covered. Return the rack to the freezer to set, at least 10 minutes. Serve directly from the freezer.

Apricot Fool Parfaits

We each had our own theory about why this traditional English dessert is called a fool. Keri thought it was because the recipe is so easy to make—just fold whipped cream into fruit puree—that any fool can do it. Greg believed that the idea was to fool you into thinking you're eating a mousse. Alas, we were both wrong. The name is actually derived from the French word *fouler*, meaning to press or to crush, and refers to the pureed fruit. Whatever the history, the appeal is clear. Deceptively simple but quite impressive looking, this layered dessert is always a hit. In Greg's restaurant experience, people love desserts served in glasses, especially fancy parfait glasses, but don't worry if you don't have any—wineglasses work just as well. **Makes 6 parfaits**

For the cake

*Baking spray with flour or unsalted butter and
    all-purpose flour for the pan*

1 Basic Cake Recipe (page 12)

½ cup apricot jam

For the parfait

1½ cups heavy cream

¼ cup fresh orange juice

1 cup apricot jam

½ recipe Whipped Cream (page 197), for garnish

Preheat the oven to 350°F and position a rack in the center. Grease the bottom of an 11 by 17-inch jelly-roll pan, line with parchment paper or aluminum foil, and grease and flour the paper.

Prepare the cake batter according to the recipe, with the following change: In Step 2, stir the apricot jam into the warm milk and butter until completely melted.

Pour the batter into the prepared pan, taking care to spread it into all corners of the pan with a rubber spatula. Bake for 15 to 20 minutes, until the surface springs back when poked with your finger and a toothpick inserted in the center of the cake comes out clean. Set the cake on a rack to cool.

When the cake is cool, run a knife around the edge of the pan and turn the cake out onto a large cutting board. Remove the parchment paper or foil. Trim ¼ inch from each side of the cake (the edges tend to be dry). Cut the cake into 1-inch squares (you'll need 18 squares).

Prepare the parfait: Whip the cream to stiff peaks (see page 7). Combine the orange juice and apricot jam in a medium bowl and stir until completely blended. Add half of the cream to the jam mixture and fold together until no streaks remain. Fold in the remaining cream.

Fill each of six parfait or wineglasses one-sixth of the way with the apricot fool. Fill the next sixth of each glass with cake, pressing it down firmly with a spoon. Continue alternating layers, pressing the cake down firmly each time, until you have six layers, ending with a layer of cake. Cover and refrigerate until set, at least 1 hour, or up to 24 hours.

Garnish each parfait with a dollop of whipped cream just before serving.

Black Bottom Cupcakes

A sophisticated take on a childhood favorite. Kids of all ages will enjoy them. **Makes 12 cupcakes**

For the filling

8 ounces cream cheese, at room temperature

3 tablespoons sugar

1 large egg white (reserve the yolk for the cake batter)

¾ cup semisweet chocolate chips

For the cupcakes

1 Basic Cake Recipe (page 12)

⅓ cup cocoa powder, whisked to remove lumps

2 ounces semisweet chocolate, chopped

Preheat the oven to 350°F and position a rack in the center. Line a standard 12-cup muffin pan with liners.

Prepare the filling: Combine the cream cheese, sugar, and egg white in the bowl of a stand mixer and beat at high speed until light and fluffy, about 3 minutes. Add the chocolate chips and mix until just combined. Set aside.

Prepare cake batter according to the recipe, with these changes: In Step 1, add cocoa to flour mixture. In Step 5, melt the chocolate in a large bowl in the microwave or in a double boiler; transfer it to a large bowl (this must be done at the last minute so the chocolate doesn't set). Add warm milk and butter to the chocolate, stir until combined, then add the chocolate to half of the batter. Stir quickly but gently until chocolate is evenly distributed. Gently fold the chocolate batter into the remaining batter until combined and no streaks remain.

Fill each muffin liner with ⅓ cup batter; it will come almost to the top. Drop a rounded tablespoon of the cream cheese mixture into each cupcake (there will be some filling left over).

Bake for 12 to 14 minutes, until a toothpick inserted in the center of a cupcake (not the filling) comes out with a few moist crumbs but is not wet. Cool the cupcakes in the tin for 5 minutes, then transfer them to a wire rack to cool. Serve warm or at room temperature.

Blackberry Petits Fours

Petit four (literally "small oven") is a catchall name for one- or two-bite cakes or treats. They are often served as part of a selection of desserts at a party, or at a tea party (real or pretend), but we also like them when we want just a little something sweet. Almost any jam can be used in this recipe, but avoid very or overly chunky preserves, which will be messy when you cut the cake. **Makes 18 petits fours**

For the cake

*Baking spray with flour or unsalted butter and
    all-purpose flour for the pan*

1 Basic Cake Recipe (page 12)

For the filling and frosting

1 cup blackberry preserves

1 cup Buttercream (page 190)

Preheat the oven to 350°F and position a rack in the center. Grease the bottom of an 11 by 17-inch jelly-roll pan, line with parchment paper or aluminum foil, and grease and flour the paper.

Prepare the cake batter according to the recipe.

Pour the batter into the prepared pan, taking care to spread it into all corners of the pan with a rubber spatula. Bake for 15 to 20 minutes, until the surface springs back when poked with your finger and a toothpick inserted in the center of the cake comes out clean. Set the cake on a rack to cool.

When the cake is cool, run a knife around the edge of the pan and turn the cake out onto a large cutting board. Remove the parchment paper or foil. Trim ¼ inch from each side of the cake (the edges tend to be dry). Cut the cake crosswise into thirds.

Prepare the filling: Melt ¾ cup of the blackberry preserves in a small saucepan over medium heat, 2 to 3 minutes. Remove from the heat.

Place one piece of the cake on a cutting board. Pour one-third of the hot jam on the cake, spreading it evenly; some jam will be absorbed into the cake. Place a second piece of cake atop the first and spread with half the remaining jam. Repeat with the remaining cake and jam. Refrigerate while you prepare the buttercream.

Mix together the remaining ¼ cup jam and the soft buttercream. Frost the cake with the buttercream. Refrigerate until set, about 1 hour.

Cut the cake into 18 squares. Serve, or refrigerate loosely covered for up to 48 hours.

Candy Cane Cupcakes

These Christmas cupcakes are festive enough for any time of the year and for any occasion—from birthday parties to summertime cookouts. **Makes 18 cupcakes**

For the cupcakes

*1 Basic Cake Recipe (page 12), minus the vanilla
    and ½ cup of the sugar*

¼ cup all-purpose flour

¼ teaspoon peppermint extract

*¾ cup powdered peppermint candy (finely grind 5 ounces
    peppermint candies or candy canes in a food processor)*

For the frosting

1 recipe White Mountain Frosting (page 192)

¼ teaspoon peppermint extract

18 peppermint candies or mini candy canes for garnish

Preheat the oven to 350°F and position a rack in the center. Line 18 standard muffin cups with liners.

Prepare the cake batter according to the recipe, with the following changes: In Step 1, add the additional ¼ cup flour to the flour mixture (1 cup total). In Step 2, omit the vanilla and add the peppermint extract. In Step 3, use only ½ cup sugar and add ½ cup of the peppermint candy powder (reserve the remainder for the frosting).

Fill each muffin liner with ⅓ cup batter; it will come almost to the top.

Bake for 12 to 14 minutes, or until the surface springs back when poked with your finger and a toothpick inserted in the center of a cupcake comes out clean. Cool the cupcakes in the tins for 5 minutes, then transfer them to a wire rack to cool completely.

While the cupcakes are cooling, prepare the frosting; stir in the reserved peppermint candy powder and the peppermint extract at the end. Frost the cupcakes liberally with icing (you may have some left over). Garnish with the peppermint candies or candy canes.

Nilla Wafer Cherry Bars

These bars have a sturdy crispy crust that makes them perfect for brown-bag lunches or picnics. **Makes sixteen 2 by 3-inch bars**

Baking spray or butter for the pan

60 Nilla Wafers

2 tablespoons unsalted butter, melted

*1 egg white (reserve the egg yolk to include in
the cake batter)*

One 16-ounce bag frozen sweet cherries, thawed and drained

1 Basic Cake Recipe (page 12)

Preheat the oven to 350°F and position a rack in the center. Grease a 9 by 13-inch baking pan.

Process the cookies in a food processor until finely ground, about 30 seconds. Add the butter and egg white and pulse until the mixture resembles coarse sand and begins to clump together, about 30 seconds. Press the mixture evenly into the bottom of the prepared pan.

Bake the crust until deep golden brown, about 10 minutes. Place on a rack to cool.

Place the cherries in a food processor. Pulse twice, so the cherries are coarsely chopped and release their juice.

Prepare the cake batter according to the recipe. Pour the cherries into the batter. They will sink to the bottom. Fold the cherries from the bottom up into the batter 3 to 4 times so that they are swirled in the batter, but do not overmix.

Pour the batter evenly over the crust. Bake for 35 minutes, or until the edges pull back from the pan and a toothpick inserted in the center of the cake comes out clean.

Cool in the pan on a rack, then cut into 16 bars.

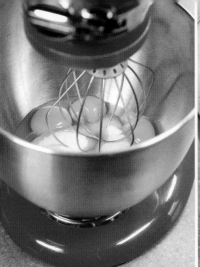

Beating the eggs and sugar

Whipping the eggs and sugar

Adding the flour

Adding the milk

Combining the batter

Folding the batter

Continuing to fold

Pouring the batter in the pan

The finished cake

Biscotti Cake (page 17)

Cheesecake (page 21)

Honey Sesame Cake (page 27)

Lemon Poppy Seed Cake (page 30)

Marble Cake (page 32)

Tarte Tatin (page 46)

Burnt Sugar Upside-Down Cake (page 51)

Honey Nut Upside-Down Cake (page 58)

Pineapple Upside-Down Cake (page 68)

Turtle Upside-Down Cake (page 73)

Amaretti Tartufi (page 76)

Apricot Fool Parfait (page 78)

Cupcakes: Black Bottom Cupcakes (page 80), Cornmeal Almond Cupcakes with Raspberry Jam (page 88), and Piña Colada Cupcakes (page 102)

Candy Cane Cupcakes (page 83)

Bars: Chocolate Chip Brownies (page 85), Chocolate Chip YPP Bars (page 86), Nilla Wafer Cherry Bars (page 84), and Fennel Semolina Raisin Bars (page 89)

Coffee and Doughnuts (page 87)

Petits Fours: Blackberry Petits Fours (page 81),
Frangipane Petits Fours (page 90), and
Butterscotch Madeleines (page 94)

Mimosa Parfaits (page 97)

Molten Chocolate Cakes (page 99)

Peanut Butter Cup Cakes (page 100)

S'mores Bars (page 104)

Sticky Toffee Pudding (page 106)

Whoopie Pies (page 108)

Apple Charlotte (page 112)

Buche de Noël (page 116)

Double Chocolate Mousse Bombe (page 120)

Frozen Blueberry Coffee Cake Terrine (page 122)

Frozen Lemon Soufflé Cake (page 124)

Jelly Roll (page 126)

Strawberry Bombe (page 137)

Summer Berry Pudding (page 139)

Boston Cream Pie (page 147)

Cappuccino Cake (page 149)

Cassata (page 154)

Coconut Cream Cake (page 156)

German Chocolate Cake (page 161)

Gingerbread Caramel Apple Cake (page 163)

Milk Chocolate Mousse Cake (page 169)

Orange Pecan Praline Cake (page 171)

Raspberry Rye Cake (page 173)

Strawberry Mousse Cake (page 177)

Tiramisu Cake (page 179)

Chocolate Chip Brownies

Adding chocolate transforms the basic recipe from a light, spongy cake to a dense and fudgy brownie. Be sure you use mini chips—big ones will sink. **Makes sixteen 2 by 3-inch bars**

Baking spray with flour, or unsalted butter
and all-purpose flour for the pan

1 Basic Cake Recipe (page 12)

8 ounces semisweet chocolate, chopped

12 ounces mini semisweet chocolate chips

Preheat the oven to 350°F and position a rack in the center. Grease and flour a 9 by 13-inch baking pan.

Prepare the cake batter according to the recipe, with the following changes: In Step 5, melt the chopped chocolate in a large bowl in the microwave, or melt the chocolate in a double boiler and then transfer it to a large bowl (this must be done at the last minute so the chocolate doesn't set). Add the warm milk and butter to the chocolate and stir until combined, then add the chocolate to half of the batter. Stir quickly but gently until the chocolate is evenly distributed. Gently fold the chocolate batter into the remaining batter until completely combined and no streaks remain. Fold 1 cup of the chocolate chips into the batter until evenly distributed.

Pour the batter into the prepared pan. Bake for 15 to 20 minutes, until the edges pull back from the pan and a toothpick inserted in the center of the cake comes out with a few moist crumbs but is not wet.

Sprinkle the remaining chips over the surface of the brownies. Don't touch the chips! They will partially melt and adhere to the brownies before setting again. Cool in the pan, then cut into 16 bars.

Chocolate Mint YPP Bars

The name comes via Keri's nephew Jonah, who, like Greg, loved York peppermint patties—so much, in fact, his parents had come up with the code "YPP." Of course, Jonah figured it out pretty quickly, but the name stuck.

Buy the jumbo bag of peppermint patties; if you use the smaller 13-ounce bag you'll only have three left over for snacking. **Makes sixteen 2 by 3-inch bars**

Baking spray or butter for the pan

One 9-ounce package chocolate wafer cookies

6 tablespoons (¾ stick) unsalted butter, melted

24 miniature York peppermint patties
  (from a 13-ounce bag; but see the headnote)

1 Basic Cake Recipe (page 12)

6 ounces semisweet chocolate, chopped

Preheat the oven to 350°F and position a rack in the center. Grease a 9 by 13-inch baking pan.

Process the cookies in a food processor until finely ground, about 30 seconds (if any large pieces remain, break them up with your fingers and then pulse a few more times). Add the butter and pulse, 3 to 5 times, until the mixture resembles wet sand. Press the crumbs evenly into the bottom of the prepared pan.

Bake the crust for 10 minutes. Arrange the peppermint patties in four rows of six each over the crust. Set aside.

Prepare the cake batter according to the recipe, with the following change: In Step 5, melt the chocolate in a large bowl in the microwave, or melt the chocolate in a double boiler and then transfer it to a large bowl (this must be done at the last minute so the chocolate doesn't set). Add the warm milk and butter to the chocolate and stir until combined, then add the chocolate to half of the batter. Stir quickly but gently until the chocolate is evenly distributed. Gently fold the chocolate batter into the remaining batter until completely combined and no streaks remain.

Pour the batter evenly over the crust. Bake for 30 to 40 minutes, or until the edges pull back from the pan and a toothpick inserted in the center of the cake comes out with a few moist crumbs but is not wet. Cool in the pan, then cut into 16 bars.

Coffee and Doughnuts

These may not look like doughnuts, but with their sweet, crunchy, cinnamon-sugar coating, they definitely taste like doughnuts. And you get coffee and doughnuts in one neat package, since the cakes are flavored with coffee. **Makes 12 "doughnuts"**

*Baking spray with flour or unsalted butter and
    all-purpose flour for the pan*

⅓ cup sugar

1 teaspoon ground cinnamon

1 Basic Cake Recipe (page 12)

¼ cup all-purpose flour

1 tablespoon instant coffee

1 tablespoon unsalted butter, melted

Preheat the oven to 350°F and position a rack in the center. Grease and flour a standard 12-cup muffin pan.

Combine the sugar and cinnamon in a large bowl and set aside.

Prepare the batter according to the recipe, with the following changes: In Step 1, add the additional ¼ cup flour to the flour mixture (1 cup total). In Step 2, dissolve the coffee in the warm milk and butter.

Fill each muffin cup with ⅓ cup batter; it will come almost to the top. Bake for 12 to 14 minutes, until the surface springs back when poked with your finger and a toothpick inserted in the center of a cupcake comes out clean.

While they are still warm, brush the tops of the cakes with melted butter. (The tops of the cakes are brushed with butter so the sugar will adhere, but the bottoms have enough moisture from steam and butter from the pan that they don't need any additional butter; you may have a little butter left over.) One at a time, gently lift each cake out of the tin and toss in the cinnamon sugar, coating it completely. Then set the cake on a wire rack.

Serve immediately with—what else?—coffee.

Cornmeal Almond Cupcakes
with Raspberry Jam

These are sophisticated cupcakes—not too sweet and slightly crunchy, the texture satisfyingly different. We prefer the crunch provided by coarse cornmeal, but if you'd like a more refined texture, use fine cornmeal. **Makes 18 cupcakes**

1 cup (about 4 ounces) sliced almonds

¼ cup cornmeal

1 Basic Cake Recipe (page 12), minus ½ cup of the flour

2 tablespoons fresh lemon juice

1 cup seedless raspberry jam

Confectioners' sugar

Preheat the oven to 350°F and position a rack in the center. Line 18 muffin cups with liners.

Process the almonds and cornmeal in a food processor until uniform, about 30 seconds. Spread on a baking sheet and toast until lightly browned and aromatic, 8 to 10 minutes. Let cool.

Prepare the cake batter according to the recipe, with the following changes: In Step 1, reduce the amount of flour to ½ cup, and add the cornmeal/almond mixture to the flour mixture. In Step 2, add the lemon juice with the vanilla.

Fill each muffin liner with ⅓ cup batter; it will come almost to the top. Bake for 12 to 14 minutes, until the surface springs back when poked with your finger and a toothpick inserted in the center of a cupcake comes out clean.

Cool the cupcakes in the tin for 5 minutes, then transfer them to a wire rack. While they are still warm, fill the cupcakes: Using the handle of a small spoon, poke a hole in the center of each cupcake. Then, using the spoon, place a scant tablespoon of jam in each hole. Again using the handle of the spoon, push the jam inside the cupcake. A small disk of jam will be visible on the top of each cupcake. Cool completely on a wire rack.

Dust the cupcakes with confectioners' sugar just before serving.

Fennel Semolina Raisin Bars

These bars are inspired by our hometown favorites, Fig Newtons (created in Newton, Massachusetts), and by Greg's travels in Italy. The semolina adds crunch, the fennel adds a floral touch, and the raisins add sweetness. The same Italian combination of flavors—fennel, semolina, and raisins—also found its way into biscotti that Greg sold in his bakery. We like the rustic quality of these bars, with their crunchy crust, chewy raisins, and soft, light cake. **Makes sixteen 2 by 3-inch bars**

Baking spray or butter for the pan

12 ounces animal crackers, about 5 cups

6 tablespoons (¾ stick) unsalted butter, melted

2 egg whites (reserve the yolks for the cake batter)

3 cups raisins

1 teaspoon fennel seeds

2 tablespoons thawed frozen orange juice concentrate

1 Basic Cake Recipe (page 12), minus ½ cup of the flour

⅓ cup semolina flour (sometimes known as pasta flour)

Preheat the oven to 350°F and position a rack in the center. Grease a 9 by 13-inch baking pan.

Process the animal crackers in a food processor until finely ground, about 30 seconds. Add the butter and 1 egg white and pulse until the mixture resembles coarse sand and begins to clump together, about 30 seconds. Press the mixture evenly into the bottom of the prepared cake pan Bake for 10 to 12 minutes, until deep golden brown (the crust may crack). Cool on a rack.

Process the raisins and fennel seeds in the food processor until finely ground, about 30 seconds. Add the orange juice concentrate and the remaining egg white and pulse 3 to 4 times, until combined. Spread the raisin mixture in an even layer over the cooled crust.

Prepare the cake batter according to the recipe, with the following change: In Step 1, reduce the amount of flour to ½ cup and add the semolina flour.

Pour the batter into the prepared pan. Bake for 30 to 40 minutes, until the edges pull back from the pan and a toothpick inserted in the center of the cake comes out clean. Set the cake on a rack to cool, then cut into 16 bars.

Frangipane Petits Fours

Sweet almond paste and tart sour cherries are common companions in many Italian desserts. The toasted pine nuts are another Italian touch, adding an almost buttery flavor and a bit of crunch. Take these along on a picnic. They're the perfect small dessert, when you want something that isn't too sweet or too rich. **Makes twenty-four 2-inch squares**

Baking spray with flour or unsalted butter and all-purpose flour for the pan

2 ounces (a scant ½ cup) pine nuts

7 ounces (about ⅔ cup) almond paste

2 tablespoons unsalted butter, cut into 4 pieces

½ cup all-purpose flour

1 large egg

1 Basic Cake Recipe (page 12)

One 14½-ounce can sour cherries, drained

Confectioners' sugar

Preheat the oven to 350°F and position a rack in the center. Grease and flour a 9 by 13-inch baking pan.

Toast the pine nuts in a small skillet over medium-high heat until golden brown, 3 to 5 minutes. Let cool.

Process the almond paste, butter, and ¼ cup of the flour in a food processor until smooth and combined, about 30 seconds, stopping to break up any large chunks of almond paste with a spoon. Add the egg and pulse 3 to 4 times, until combined. Transfer to a medium bowl and set aside.

Prepare the cake batter according to the recipe, with the following changes: In Step 1, add the remaining ¼ cup flour to the flour mixture (1 cup total). In Step 5, add about 1 cup of the batter to the almond paste mixture and stir to combine. Add the almond mixture to the remaining batter and fold gently to combine.

Pour the batter into the prepared pan. Scatter the cherries evenly over the surface of the cake (they will sink). Sprinkle with the pine nuts.

Bake for 25 to 30 minutes, until the edges pull back from the pan and a toothpick inserted in the center of the cake comes out clean. Set the cake on a rack to cool.

When the cake is cool, cut into 24 pieces. Dust with confectioners' sugar just before serving.

Individual Berry Shortcakes

Traditionally shortcake is very dense and dry, but this light and airy version is perfect for a lazy summer evening dessert. The berries and sugar make a sweet syrup that is soaked up by the sponge cake, giving it a rich fruity flavor. It's an ideal make-ahead dessert, since all the components can be prepared early in the afternoon and then assembled just before serving. Be sure to use the freshest, ripest berries you can find. **Serves 6**

Baking spray with flour or unsalted butter and
all-purpose flour for the pan

1 Basic Cake Recipe (page 12)

Confectioners' sugar

1 recipe Whipped Cream (page 197)

4 cups mixed berries (if using strawberries, hull and slice them)

2 tablespoons sugar

1 teaspoon fresh lemon juice

Preheat the oven to 350°F and position a rack in the center. Lightly grease the bottom of an 11 by 17-inch jelly-roll pan, line with parchment paper or aluminum foil, and grease and flour the paper.

Prepare the cake batter according to the recipe.

Pour the batter into the prepared pan, taking care to spread it into all corners of the pan with a rubber spatula. Bake for 15 to 20 minutes, until the surface springs back when poked with your finger and a toothpick inserted in the center of the cake comes out clean. Set the cake on a rack to cool.

When the cake is cool, run a knife around the edge of the pan and turn the cake out onto a large cutting board. Remove the parchment paper or foil. Cut out 12 rounds of cake with a 3½- to 4-inch biscuit cutter. Transfer 6 rounds to a rack and sprinkle with confectioners' sugar.

Prepare the whipped cream and refrigerate. Combine the berries, sugar, and lemon juice in a large bowl and mash with a potato masher or fork until the mixture is juicy and syrupy but some pieces of berry remain (how much you have to mash will depend on how ripe your berries are—ripe berries break down very quickly, while firmer berries take a little work).

Place the remaining 6 rounds of cake on six dessert plates. Spoon about $\frac{1}{4}$ cup of the whipped cream on top of each cake. Divide the berry mixture among the cakes and top each with another $\frac{1}{4}$ cup whipped cream. Cover with the sugared rounds of cake (we like to place them at a slight angle). Serve immediately.

Butterscotch Madeleines

Considered a cookie but definitely more cakelike in nature, sweet, light madeleines are a classic accompaniment to tea and are often served warm at the end of a meal. A special madeleine pan, available at cookware stores, is necessary for these. If you like the easy elegance of these tea cakes, we recommend investing in two pans (or even three). These cook quickly, and the batter will hold, but you should refrigerate it between batches. **Makes about 36 madeleines**

> *Baking spray with flour or unsalted butter and*
>   *all-purpose flour for the pan*
>
> *1 Basic Cake Recipe (page 12), minus the granulated sugar*
>
> *¼ cup all-purpose flour*
>
> *1 cup packed dark brown sugar*

Preheat the oven to 400°F and position a rack in the center. Generously grease and flour two or three madeleine pans (or one, if that's all you have).

Prepare the cake batter according to the recipe, with the following changes: In Step 1, add the additional ¼ cup flour to the flour mixture (1 cup total). In Step 3, replace the granulated sugar with the dark brown sugar.

Fill the madeleine molds halfway, using about 1 tablespoon batter for each. Bake for 6 to 8 minutes, until the edges are brown but the tops are still light.

Immediately turn the madeleines out onto a wire rack to cool. Repeat with the remaining batter, if necessary.

Serve warm.

Milky Way Cupcakes

This cupcake is reminiscent of a Milky Way, but ever so much better. The flavors are similar, but the chocolate is richer, the mousse lighter, and the homemade caramel glaze sweet and shiny. **Makes 12 cupcakes**

For the filling
1 recipe Milk Chocolate Mousse (page 186)

For the cake
1 Basic Cake Recipe (page 12)

⅓ cup cocoa powder, whisked to remove lumps

2 ounces semisweet chocolate, chopped

For the glaze
1 recipe Caramel Glaze (page 193)

Prepare the mousse and place it in the refrigerator to set.

Preheat the oven to 350°F and position a rack in the center. Line a standard 12-cup muffin pan with liners.

Prepare the cake batter according to the recipe, with the following changes: In Step 1, add the cocoa to the flour mixture. In Step 5, melt the chocolate in a large bowl in the microwave, or melt the chocolate in a double boiler and then transfer it to a large bowl (this must be done at the last minute so the chocolate doesn't set). Add the warm milk and butter to the chocolate and stir until combined, then add the chocolate to half of the batter. Stir quickly but gently until the chocolate is evenly distributed. Gently fold the chocolate batter into the remaining batter until completely combined and no streaks remain.

Fill each muffin liner with ⅓ cup batter; it will come almost to the top. Bake for 12 to 14 minutes, until the surface springs back when poked with your finger and a toothpick inserted in the center of a cupcake comes out with a few moist crumbs but is not wet.

Cool the cupcakes in the tin for 5 minutes, then transfer them to a wire rack to cool.

When the cakes are cool, prepare the glaze. While the glaze is still warm (but not bubbling), coat the cupcakes: Hold a cupcake upside down over the glaze and gently dip it into the glaze, completely submerging the top but not any of the paper liner. Lift the cupcake and allow the excess glaze to drain into the bowl, then turn the cupcake right side up and return to the rack. Repeat with the remaining cupcakes (you will have some glaze left over). Let stand until set, about 10 minutes.

Once the glaze is set, fill the cupcakes: With a serrated knife, cut the top from each cupcake, just above the paper liner. Place 2 tablespoons mousse on each cupcake and replace the tops, pushing them down gently to spread the filling to the sides. Serve immediately.

Mimosa Parfaits

What's better than a mimosa with brunch? How about a mimosa for dessert? These are a festive do-ahead dessert. They'll keep for several days in the freezer, so they're great for entertaining–prepare them one night, and they're ready for brunch the next morning. You will only need half of the cake for these; frost or glaze the rest and cut it into squares for a simple snack. **Makes 6 parfaits**

1 recipe Champagne Granita (page 182)

For the cake

Baking spray with flour or unsalted butter and
*   all-purpose flour for the pan*

1 Basic Cake Recipe (page 12)

1 teaspoon grated orange zest

1 recipe Whipped Cream (page 197)

Prepare the granita.

Preheat the oven to 350°F and position a rack in the center. Grease the bottom of an 11 by 17-inch jelly-roll pan, line with parchment paper or aluminum foil, and grease and flour the paper.

Prepare the cake batter according to the recipe, with the following change: Before mixing the batter, combine the orange zest and the ¾ cup sugar for the cake in a food processor and process until well blended, about 10 seconds; the mixture will resemble wet sand. In Step 3, whip the orange sugar with the eggs and yolks.

Pour the batter into the prepared pan. Bake for 15 to 20 minutes, until the surface springs back when poked with your finger and a toothpick inserted in the center of the cake comes out clean. Set the cake on a rack to cool.

When the cake is cool, run a knife around the edge of the pan and turn the cake out onto a large cutting board. Remove the parchment paper or foil and trim ¼ inch from each side of the cake (the edges tend to be dry). Cut the cake in half and cut one half into 1-inch squares. (You won't need the rest of the cake; feel free to snack on it.)

Prepare the whipped cream. Combine half of it with the cake squares in a large bowl. Refrigerate the remaining whipped cream until needed.

Fill six champagne flutes one-fifth of the way with the cake mixture, pressing it down firmly. Fill the next fifth of each glass with granita. Continue alternating the layers, pressing the cake down firmly, until you have five layers, ending with a layer of cake. Freeze until set, about 1 hour, or up to 48 hours.

Garnish the parfaits with the reserved whipped cream just before serving.

Molten Chocolate Cakes

These must be served warm so the filling oozes out when you cut into it. If you have any leftovers, though, you can reheat them in the microwave. If you use Baker's chocolate, cut each square into quarters for the filling. If you use a thinner chocolate bar, such as Ghirardelli, you'll have to stack small pieces to create a 1-inch chunk that will fit inside each cake. **Makes 12 cakes**

For the cake

Baking spray with flour or unsalted butter and
    all-purpose flour for the pan

1 Basic Cake Recipe (page 12)

¼ cup all-purpose flour

8 ounces semisweet chocolate, chopped

For the filling

3 ounces semisweet chocolate, divided into twelve
    1-inch-square portions

Preheat the oven to 350°F and position a rack in the center. Grease and flour a standard 12-cup muffin pan.

Prepare the cake batter according to the recipe, with the following changes: In Step 1, add the additional ¼ cup flour to the flour mixture (1 cup total). In Step 5, melt the chocolate in a large bowl in the microwave, or melt the chocolate in a double boiler and then transfer it to a large bowl (this must be done at the last minute so the chocolate doesn't set). Add the warm milk and butter to the chocolate and stir until combined, then add the chocolate to half of the batter. Stir quickly but gently until the chocolate is evenly distributed. Gently fold the chocolate batter into the remaining batter until completely combined and no streaks remain.

Fill each muffin tin with ⅓ cup batter; it will come almost to the top (there may be leftover batter). Press a chocolate square into each cupcake so it is level with the surface of the batter.

Bake for 10 minutes, or until the edges pull back from the pan and a toothpick inserted in the edge of the cake comes out with a few moist crumbs but is not wet. Let the cakes set on a wire rack for 5 minutes, then turn out onto serving plates. Serve immediately with Whipped Cream (page 197) or Vanilla Ice Cream (page 184).

Peanut Butter Cup Cakes

Keri's brother-in-law Andy is a peanut butter fanatic. He'd rather have a spoonful of peanut butter for dessert than almost anything else. When he came to dinner at a restaurant Keri was working at several years ago, she had the pastry chef prepare a special peanut butter mousse in chocolate cups. When the waiter brought the dessert out, Andy was so touched, he cried. He then proceeded to eat all the peanut butter mousse and passed the chocolate cups to Keri's sister. These cupcakes are for Andy. **Makes 12 cupcakes**

For the filling
1 recipe Peanut Butter Mousse (page 188)

For the cake
1 Basic Cake Recipe (page 12)

⅓ cup cocoa powder, whisked to remove lumps

2 ounces semisweet chocolate, chopped

Prepare the mousse and place it in the refrigerator to set.

Preheat the oven to 350°F and position a rack in the center. Line a standard 12-cup muffin pan with liners.

Prepare the cake batter according to the recipe, with the following changes: In Step 1, add the cocoa to the flour mixture. In Step 5, melt the chocolate in a large bowl in the microwave, or melt the chocolate in a double boiler and then transfer it to a large bowl (this must be done at the last minute so the chocolate doesn't set). Add the warm milk and butter to the chocolate and stir until combined, then add the chocolate to half of the batter. Stir quickly but gently until the chocolate is evenly distributed. Gently fold the chocolate batter into the remaining batter until completely combined and no streaks remain.

Fill each muffin liner with ⅓ cup batter; it will come almost to the top. Bake for 13 to 15 minutes, or until the surface springs back when poked with your finger and a toothpick inserted in the center of a cupcake comes out with a few moist crumbs but is not wet.

Cool the cupcakes in the tin for 5 minutes, then transfer them to a wire rack to cool.

When the cupcakes are cool, fill them: With a small knife, cut out a shallow circle of cake from the center of each cupcake and set aside (see illustration). Divide the mousse among the cupcakes, then place the reserved cake atop the mousse.

Serve, or store the cupcakes in the refrigerator. Remove about 20 minutes before serving to take the chill off.

Piña Colada Cupcakes

Yes, we like piña coladas...and cupcakes! These are a very adult cupcake, with the rich piña colada flavors of coconut, pineapple, and rum that will transport you to the beach. **Makes 18 cupcakes**

For the filling

1 tablespoon cornstarch

½ cup heavy cream

2 tablespoons coconut rum or dark rum, optional

2 tablespoons sugar

1 cup canned crushed pineapple, with juice

2 cups sweetened shredded coconut

For the cake

1 Basic Cake Recipe (page 12)

2 tablespoons coconut rum or plain rum, optional

Preheat the oven to 350°F and position a rack in the center. Line two standard 12-cup muffin pans with liners.

Dissolve the cornstarch in the cream in a medium heavy-bottomed saucepan. Add the remaining filling ingredients and bring the mixture to a boil, stirring occasionally. Cook for 1 minute, stirring. Remove from the heat and pour into a bowl. Refrigerate until set, about 30 minutes.

Spread the coconut in an even layer on a baking sheet and toast for 8 to 10 minutes, until lightly browned, with some white spots. Place on a rack to cool.

Set aside ½ cup of the toasted coconut for garnish. Grind the remaining 1½ cups coconut in a food processor until fine, about 30 seconds.

Prepare the cake batter according to the recipe, with the following changes: In Step 1, add the ground coconut to the flour mixture. In Step 2, add the rum, if using, with the vanilla.

Fill each muffin liner with ⅓ cup batter; it will come almost to the top of the liner. Bake for 13 to 15 minutes, until the surface springs back when poked with your finger and a toothpick inserted in the center of a cupcake comes out clean.

Cool the cupcakes in the tins for 5 minutes, then transfer them to a wire rack to cool.

When the cupcakes are cool, fill them: With a small knife, cut out a shallow circle of cake from the center of each cupcake (see the illustration on page 101) and discard (or enjoy as a baker's treat). Divide the filling among the cupcakes and top with the reserved toasted coconut. Serve immediately.

S'Mores Bars

While no one knows exactly when s'mores were invented, there are recipes for "some mores" in a 1927 Girl Scouts camping recipe book. Graham crackers, chocolate, and marshmallows are a uniquely American combination (think Scooter Pies and Mallomars). With real s'mores, timing is everything. Toast the marshmallow too long, and it will burn or, worse, fall into the fire. But don't toast it enough, and it won't properly melt the chocolate. Here, we put the same great flavor combination in a rich, chocolaty brownie. No need to worry about burning or losing marshmallows. **Makes sixteen 2 by 3-inch bars**

Baking spray or butter for the pan

7 to 10 whole graham crackers, plus 1 cup graham crackers crushed into pieces (about ½ inch; because size varies by brand, the number of crackers you need will vary)

1 cup milk chocolate chips

2 cups mini marshmallows

1 Basic Cake Recipe (page 12)

6 ounces semisweet chocolate, chopped

Preheat the oven to 350°F and position a rack in the center. Grease a 9 by 13-inch baking pan.

Line the bottom of the prepared pan with the whole graham crackers, breaking them if necessary to make an even layer with no overlap. Sprinkle the graham crackers with ½ cup of the milk chocolate chips and 1 cup of the mini marshmallows; set aside. Combine the graham cracker pieces, the remaining ½ cup chips, and the remaining 1 cup marshmallows in a bowl and set aside.

Prepare the cake batter according to the recipe, with the following change: In Step 5, melt the chocolate in a large bowl in the microwave, or melt the chocolate in a double boiler and then transfer it to a large bowl (this must be done at the last minute so the chocolate doesn't set). Add the warm milk and butter to the chocolate and stir until combined, then add the chocolate to half of the batter. Stir quickly but gently until the chocolate is evenly distributed. Gently fold the chocolate batter into the remaining batter until completely combined and no streaks remain.

Pour the batter evenly over the chocolate and marshmallows in the baking pan. Bake for 10 minutes, or until the cake is just beginning to set. Sprinkle the reserved graham cracker mixture over the top of the cake. Bake for 10 to 12 minutes longer, until the marshmallows begin to brown and a toothpick inserted in the center of the cake (not the topping!) comes out with some moist crumbs of cake but is not wet.

Cool in the pan, then cut into 16 bars.

Sticky Toffee Pudding

Although this isn't a pudding, and there isn't any toffee in it, the name of this traditional dessert is actually quite appropriate. In England, where the dessert originated, all sweets are called puddings. The sticky part comes from the sweet, sticky dates that make the cake unbelievably moist, and the toffee is in the sauce. Sticky toffee pudding is all about the sauce—the cake is essentially a vehicle for the sauce. **Serves 10 to 12**

For the cake

*Baking spray with flour or unsalted butter and
  all-purpose flour for the pan*

1 pound (about 2 cups firmly packed) dates

*1 Basic Cake Recipe (page 12), minus ½ cup
  of the granulated sugar*

½ cup packed dark brown sugar

For the sauce

2 cups heavy cream

¾ cup packed dark brown sugar

2 tablespoons unsalted butter

Preheat the oven to 350°F and position a rack in the center. Grease and flour two standard 12-cup muffin pans.

Combine the dates and 1 cup water in a small saucepan over medium-high heat and bring to a boil. Reduce the heat to low and simmer until almost all the liquid is absorbed (you will see a thin smear of liquid on the bottom of the pot), 10 to 15 minutes.

Transfer the dates to a food processor and puree until smooth, about 20 seconds. Scrape into a small bowl.

Prepare the cake batter according to the recipe, with the following changes: In Step 3, replace ½ cup of the granulated sugar with the dark brown sugar. In Step 5, add the warm milk and butter to the dates and stir until combined, then add the date mixture to half of the batter. Stir quickly but gently until the dates are evenly distributed. Gently fold the date batter into the remaining batter until completely combined and no streaks remain.

Divide the batter among the prepared pans. You will get 20 to 22 cakes. Bake for 13 to 15 minutes, until the edges pull back from the pan and a toothpick inserted in the center of a cake comes out clean.

While the cakes are baking, prepare the sauce: Combine all the ingredients in a medium saucepan over medium-high heat. Stir to dissolve the sugar. Bring to a boil, then reduce the heat to low and simmer until thickened, 15 to 20 minutes.

Serve the cakes warm. Arrange 2 cakes on each plate and top with ¼ cup sauce. If there are any leftovers, reheat the sauce before serving.

Whoopie Pies

Many believe that whoopie pies (which aren't really a pie at all) originated with the Pennsylvania Dutch, who used bits of leftover batter to make small treats for the kids. Our version is far better than the dry cakes and cloyingly sweet filling we remember from our youth. They're so easy to make and fun to eat, they're great for parties. And they aren't too sweet at all, which makes them appealing to kids and adults alike. **Makes 6 "pies"**

For the cake

*Baking spray with flour or unsalted butter and
all-purpose flour for the pan*

1 Basic Cake Recipe (page 12)

¼ cup cocoa powder, whisked to remove lumps

4 ounces semisweet chocolate, chopped

For the filling

1 recipe White Mountain Frosting (page 192)

Preheat the oven to 350°F and position a rack in the center. Grease the bottom of an 11 by 17-inch jelly-roll pan, line with parchment paper or aluminum foil, and grease and flour the paper.

Prepare the cake batter according to the recipe, with the following changes: In Step 1, add the cocoa powder to the flour mixture. In Step 5, melt the chocolate in a large bowl in the microwave, or melt the chocolate in a double boiler and then transfer it to a large bowl (this must be done at the last minute so the chocolate doesn't set). Add the warm milk and butter to the chocolate and stir until combined, then add the chocolate to half of the batter. Stir quickly but gently until the chocolate is evenly distributed. Gently fold the chocolate batter into the remaining batter until completely combined and no streaks remain.

Pour the batter into the prepared pan, taking care to spread it into all corners of the pan with a rubber spatula. Bake for 15 to 20 minutes, until the surface springs back when poked with your finger and a toothpick inserted in the center of the cake comes out with a few moist crumbs but is not wet. Set the cake on a rack to cool.

When the cake is cool, run a knife around the edge of the pan and turn the cake out onto a large cutting board. Remove the parchment paper or foil. Cut out 12 rounds of cake with a 3½- to 4-inch biscuit cutter. Save the scraps for a nibble.

Prepare the frosting.

Arrange 6 cake rounds on a serving platter. Spread the frosting evenly on each cake. Top with the remaining 6 rounds. Press the top of each whoopie pie down gently so the filling spreads to the edges. Serve immediately. Refrigerate any leftovers.

Specialty Desserts, Roulades, and Frozen Treats

These are special-occasion desserts, the ones where all the stops are pulled out. Elegant bombes. Striking charlottes. Homemade ice cream cakes. These cakes may require a bit more work and assembly, but the results are more than worth it.

Many of these cakes need to sit overnight in the refrigerator or freezer, so be sure to read the directions through before starting so you're not surprised at 5:00 p.m. with a dessert that won't be ready until midnight.

We like to keep frozen desserts on hand and just take off a slice or two as needed. While this wouldn't work for a special party, it is great for last-minute company or a weeknight dessert for the family.

Apple Charlotte

The rustic simplicity of this cake is the very essence of autumn. You will need to bake two sheets of cake; because the filling is so wet and heavy it needs two layers of cake to support it. If you don't have two jelly-roll pans, just make one recipe of batter at a time. **Serves 10 to 12**

For the cake

Baking spray with flour or unsalted butter and all-purpose flour for the pan

2 Basic Cake Recipes (page 12)

1 tablespoon ground cinnamon

For the filling

4½ cups applesauce

3 large eggs

¼ cup all-purpose flour

Pinch of salt

Preheat the oven to 350°F and position two racks in the upper and lower thirds of the oven. Lightly grease the bottom of two 11 by 17-inch jelly-roll pans, line them with parchment paper or aluminum foil, and grease and flour the paper.

Prepare the double batch of cake batter according to the recipe, with the following change: In Step 1, add the cinnamon to the flour mixture.

Pour the batter into the prepared pans, taking care to spread it into all corners of the pans with a rubber spatula. Bake for 15 to 20 minutes, until the surface springs back when poked with your finger and a toothpick inserted in the center of the cakes comes out clean. Set the cakes on racks to cool.

When the cakes are cool, run a knife around the edges of the pans and turn each cake out onto a large cutting board. Remove the parchment paper or foil. Trim ¼ inch from each side of each cake (the edges tend to be dry). Cut out two 8-inch disks from one cake. Cut out a 10-inch disk from the other cake, then cut the rest of the cake into 3-inch-wide strips.

Grease a 9-inch springform pan and lay both 8-inch circles in the pan. Cut the 3-inch strips crosswise into 2½-inch pieces and arrange them around the side of the pan, overlapping them slightly (you will need about 17 pieces).

Prepare the filling: Combine all the ingredients in a medium saucepan over medium-high heat and bring to a boil, stirring often. Cook 1 minute longer. Pour into the prepared pan.

Cut the 10-inch disk of cake into 12 equal wedges. Place the wedges on top of the filling, overlapping them slightly (see illustration).

Cover the cake with a large piece of greased aluminum foil and crimp the edges tightly. Bake for 1 hour, or until the filling is set and the edges of the cake are brown and toasted (carefully lift an edge of the foil to check). Remove the foil and set the cake on a rack to cool for about 15 minutes.

Remove the springform ring. Using a large spatula (or two), transfer the cake to a serving platter. Serve warm with Vanilla Ice Cream (page 184) or Whipped Cream (page 197).

Banana Cream Roulade

A rolled cake always reminds us of the Swiss rolls we ate as kids. When you cut into it and see the spiral slices, it's a fun surprise. Don't be intimidated by roulades—they're just jelly rolls without the jelly. They look impressive, but they're a lot easier to make than they may seem. **Serves 8 to 10**

For the cake

*Baking spray with flour, or unsalted butter
and all-purpose flour for the pan*

2 medium ripe bananas

1 tablespoon fresh lemon juice

1 Basic Cake Recipe (page 12)

For the filling

1 recipe Whipped Cream (page 197)

1 medium ripe banana, diced

Confectioners' sugar

Preheat the oven to 350°F and position a rack in the center. Grease the bottom of an 11 by 17-inch jelly-roll pan, line with parchment paper or aluminum foil, and grease and flour the paper.

Puree the bananas with the lemon juice in a food processor until smooth. Measure out 1 cup puree (discard the rest).

Prepare the cake batter according to the recipe, with the following change: In Step 2, stir the banana puree into the warm milk and butter until combined.

Pour the batter into the prepared pan, taking care to spread it into all corners of the pan with a rubber spatula. Bake for 15 to 20 minutes, until the surface springs back when poked with your finger and a toothpick inserted in the center of the cake comes out clean.

Run a knife around the edge of the pan and immediately turn the cake out onto a rack covered with a clean dish towel to cool.

When the cake is cool, slide it, on the dish towel, onto the countertop, remove the parchment paper or foil, and trim ¼ inch from each side of the cake (the edges tend to be dry).

Prepare the whipped cream. Fold the diced banana into the cream until evenly distributed.

Arrange the cake so that a long side is directly in front of you. Spread the whipped cream in an even layer over the cake, going right up to the edges on the long side directly in front of you and the two short sides but only to within 1 inch of the top. Gently roll up the cake from the long side near you, using the dish towel to lift the cake and your fingers to tuck in the edge (see the illustration on page 8) and ending with the seam side down. Use the dish towel to help press the cake into an even roll. Remove the dish towel and transfer the roulade to a platter.

Chill the roulade for at least 1 hour or up to 48 hours. Dust with confectioners' sugar just before serving.

Bûche de Noël

This traditional French Christmas cake starts with a roulade filled with coffee buttercream, which is decorated with chocolate buttercream to resemble a festive Yule log. **Serves 8 to 10**

For the cake

Baking spray with flour or unsalted butter and
  all-purpose flour for the pan

1 Basic Cake Recipe (page 12)

⅓ cup cocoa powder, whisked to remove lumps

For the filling and frosting

1 recipe Chocolate Buttercream (page 190)

1 recipe Buttercream (page 190)

2 tablespoons instant coffee

1 tablespoon dark rum or warm water

Preheat the oven to 350°F and position a rack in the center. Grease the bottom of an 11 by 17-inch jelly-roll pan, line with parchment paper or aluminum foil, and grease and flour the paper.

Prepare the batter according to the recipe, with the following change: In Step 1, add the cocoa powder to the flour mixture.

Pour the cake batter into the prepared pan, taking care to spread it into all corners of the pan with a rubber spatula. Bake for 15 to 20 minutes, until the surface springs back when poked with your finger and a toothpick inserted in the center of the cake comes out clean.

Run a knife around the edge of the pan and immediately turn the cake out onto a wire rack covered with a clean dish towel. Set aside to cool while you prepare the buttercreams.

Leave the plain buttercream in the mixer bowl. Stir the instant coffee into the rum until completely dissolved. Add the coffee mixture to the plain buttercream and mix on high speed until combined.

Slide the cake, on the dish towel, onto the countertop and remove the parchment paper or foil. Trim ¼ inch from each side of the cake (the edges tend to be dry).

Arrange the cake so that a long side is directly in front of you. Spread the coffee buttercream in an even layer over the cake, going right up to the edges on the long side directly in front of you and the two short sides but only to within 1 inch of the top. Gently roll up the cake from the long side near you, using the dish towel to lift the cake and your fingers to tuck in the edge (see the illustration on page 8) and ending with the seam side down. Use the dish towel to help press the cake into an even roll. Remove the dish towel and transfer the roulade to a serving platter. Refrigerate the cake for at least 30 minutes. Set the chocolate buttercream aside.

Frost the roulade with the chocolate buttercream, reserving about ½ cup for touch-ups. Cut off a 3-inch piece from one end at a 45-degree angle (illustration 1). Cut off a thin slice from the other end at the same angle; eat or discard this thin slice. Attach the large piece, flat side down, on top of the roulade in the center, using the buttercream as adhesive; press down slightly to adhere it to the cake. Using the reserved chocolate buttercream, frost the end of the "stump" (illustration 2). Using a fork, gently trace lines in the buttercream so that it resembles tree bark (illustration 3).

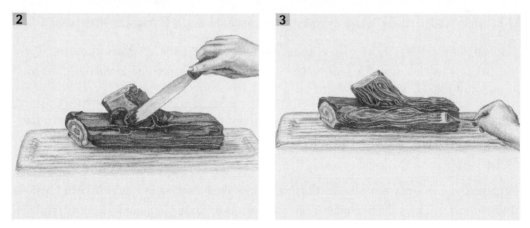

Chill for at least 1 hour, or up to 48 hours, before serving.

Chocolate Hazelnut Roulade

While we wish we could take credit for the delicious pairing of chocolate and hazelnuts, this is only our take on a classic combination that is very popular in Europe. Toasting really brings out the sweet hazelnut flavor, which in turn pairs wonderfully with the rich chocolate. **Serves 8 to 10**

For the cake

Baking spray with flour or unsalted butter and all-purpose flour for the pan

½ cup chopped hazelnuts (peeled or unpeeled; about 2 ounces)

1 Basic Cake Recipe (page 12), minus ¼ cup of the granulated sugar

¼ cup packed dark brown sugar

For the filling and frosting

Double recipe Chocolate Buttercream (page 190)

½ cup chopped hazelnuts (peeled or unpeeled; about 2 ounces)

Preheat the oven to 350°F and position a rack in the center. Grease the bottom of an 11 by 17-inch jelly-roll pan, line with parchment paper or aluminum foil, and grease the paper.

Toast all the hazelnuts, both for the cake and the filling: Spread the hazelnuts in an even layer on a baking sheet and toast for 5 to 7 minutes, until lightly browned and aromatic. Place on a rack to cool.

When the nuts are cool, grind in a food processor until fine, about 20 seconds. Transfer half of the hazelnuts to a small bowl and set aside. Leave the remaining hazelnuts in the food processor.

Prepare the cake batter according to the recipe, with the following changes: In Step 1, grind the flour mixture with the hazelnuts in the food processor until combined. In Step 3, replace ¼ of the granulated sugar with the dark brown sugar.

Pour the batter into the prepared pan, taking care to spread it into all corners of the pan with a rubber spatula. Bake for 15 to 20 minutes, until the surface springs back when poked with your finger and a toothpick inserted in the center of the cake comes out clean.

Run a knife around the edge of the pan and immediately turn the cake out onto a rack covered with a clean dish towel. Set aside to cool.

Prepare the buttercream. Stir the reserved hazelnuts into the buttercream.

When it is cool, slide the cake, on the dish towel, onto the countertop and remove the parchment paper or foil. Trim ¼ inch from each side of the cake (the edges tend to be dry).

Arrange the cake so that a long side is directly in front of you. Spread half of the buttercream in an even layer over the cake, going right up to the edges on the long side directly in front of you and the two short sides but only to within 1 inch of the top. Gently roll up the cake from the long side near you, using the dish towel to lift the cake and your fingers to tuck in the edge (see the illustration on page 8) and ending with the seam side down. Use the dish towel to help press the cake into an even roll. Remove the dish towel and transfer the roulade to a serving platter. Refrigerate for at least 30 minutes. Set the buttercream aside.

Frost the roulade with the remaining buttercream. Chill for at least 1 hour, and up to 48 hours, before serving.

Double Chocolate Mousse Bombe

This is a spectacular special-occasion dessert, impressive and sinfully rich. Though the term "bombe" was originally reserved for dome-shaped ice cream cakes or frozen desserts, today it is used for almost any bowl-shaped dessert. The glaze will lose its luster when refrigerated, so don't glaze the bombe until about 30 minutes before you're ready to serve it. But do refrigerate leftovers; the glaze will have a matte rather than shiny finish. **Serves 8**

For the cake

*Baking spray with flour or unsalted butter and
   all-purpose flour for the pan*

1 Basic Cake Recipe (page 12)

⅓ cup cocoa powder, whisked to remove lumps

For the filling and frosting

1 recipe Milk Chocolate Mousse (page 186)

1 recipe Dark Chocolate Mousse (page 183)

1 recipe Chocolate Glaze (page 194)

1 ounce chocolate (any kind) for shavings (see page 10), optional

Preheat the oven to 350°F and position a rack in the center. Grease the bottom of an 11 by 17-inch jelly-roll pan, line with parchment paper or aluminum foil, and grease and flour the paper.

Prepare the cake batter according to the recipe, with the following change: In Step 1, add the cocoa to the flour mixture.

Pour the batter into the prepared pan, taking care to spread it into all corners of the pan with a rubber spatula. Bake for 15 to 20 minutes, until the surface springs back when poked with your finger and a toothpick inserted in the center of the cake comes out clean. Set the cake on a rack to cool.

Line a 1½-quart bowl (we like the 1.5L Pyrex) with plastic wrap, leaving plenty of overhang on the sides. (When the cake is finished, you will use the plastic wrap to remove the cake from the pan.)

When the cake is cool, run a knife around the edge of the pan and turn the cake out onto a large cutting board. Remove the parchment paper or foil. Trim ¼ inch from each side of the cake (the edges tend to be dry). Cut the cake into pieces according to the diagram on page 8. Line the bowl with the cake according to the illustrations on page 8, trimming any excess that comes above the rim of the bowl.

Once the bowl is lined, prepare the milk chocolate mousse. Pour the unchilled mousse directly into the cake-lined bowl and tap the bowl gently to distribute the mousse evenly. Place in the freezer while you prepare the dark chocolate mousse.

Pour the unchilled dark chocolate mousse directly over the milk chocolate mousse. Place the large circle of cake directly on top of the dark chocolate mousse and press gently. Pull the plastic wrap over the top to cover.

Refrigerate the bombe until set, at least 2 hours, or up to 48 hours.

When the bombe is set, prepare the glaze. Set the glaze aside to cool slightly while you turn out the bombe: Peel back the plastic wrap from the cake and turn the cake out onto a rack set over a baking sheet; you may have to pull slightly on the plastic wrap to get the bowl off. Gently remove the plastic wrap and discard.

Pour most of the glaze over the center of the bombe, letting it run down the sides. Using an offset spatula, spread the glaze in an even layer over the bombe, using the reserved glaze to fill any holes. Try to let the glaze do most of the work—the less you use the spatula, the less streaky the glaze will be. While the glaze is still wet, decorate the bombe with chocolate shavings, if desired. Let stand at room temperature to set, about 30 minutes.

Use a large spatula to transfer the bombe to a serving plate. Serve immediately with Whipped Cream (page 197) and fresh raspberries.

Frozen Blueberry Coffee Cake Terrine

Here all the elements of a blueberry coffee cake are transformed into a frozen dessert. The layers create a very elegant presentation that's perfect after a summer dinner. There will be some extra cake and jam, so do what Greg does: serve dessert canapés. Pass around bites of cake and jam when guests arrive as a preview of the dessert to come. **Serves 6 to 8**

For the cake

Baking spray with flour or unsalted butter and all-purpose flour for the pan

1 Basic Cake Recipe (page 12), minus ½ cup of the granulated sugar

1 teaspoon ground cinnamon

½ cup packed dark brown sugar

For the filling and topping

One 12-ounce jar blueberry jam

1 recipe Vanilla Ice Cream (page 184) or ½ gallon store-bought vanilla ice cream, softened

2 tablespoons grated lemon zest

Preheat the oven to 350°F and position a rack in the center. Grease the bottom of an 11 by 17-inch jelly-roll pan, line with parchment paper or aluminum foil, and grease and flour the paper.

Prepare the cake batter according to the recipe, with the following changes: In Step 1, add the cinnamon to the flour mixture. In Step 3, replace ½ cup of the granulated sugar with the dark brown sugar.

Pour the batter into the prepared pan, taking care to spread it into all corners of the pan with a rubber spatula. Bake for 15 to 20 minutes, until the surface springs back when poked with your finger and a toothpick inserted in the center of the cake comes out clean. Set the cake on a rack to cool.

Line a 9 by 5-inch loaf pan with plastic wrap, leaving plenty of overhang on the sides. (When the cake is finished, you will use the plastic wrap to remove the cake from the pan.)

When the cake is cool, run a knife around the edge of the pan and turn the cake out onto a cutting board. Remove the parchment paper or foil. Trim ¼ inch from each side of the cake (the edges tend to be dry).

Arrange the cake so that a long side is directly in front of you and cut the cake crosswise into thirds. Spread one-third of the jam on each strip of cake.

Combine the ice cream and lemon zest in a large bowl, stirring until well blended. If the ice cream is very soft, freeze until it holds its shape and is no longer soft.

Place one cake strip in the loaf pan, trimming the sides so that it fits snugly. Top with half the ice cream and spread in an even layer. Place another trimmed cake strip on top of the ice cream, pressing it down slightly. Spread the remaining ice cream on top of the cake. Place the last strip of trimmed cake, jam side down, on top of the ice cream and press down slightly. Pull the plastic wrap over the top to cover. Freeze until set, at least 1 hour, or up to 1 week.

To unmold the terrine, peel back the plastic wrap and invert the terrine onto a cutting board. Pull down on the plastic wrap as you lift up the pan and remove it. Slice the terrine and serve immediately.

Frozen Lemon Soufflé Cake

We love this showstopper of a recipe. Light and refreshing, it's great for formal dinner parties in warm weather. You will need a springform pan for this recipe. Serve it with Whipped Cream (page 197). The cake will keep in the freezer for up to 1 week; cut slices and snack on it all week long. **Serves 10 to 12**

For the filling

1½ teaspoons grated lemon zest

1 cup fresh lemon juice (from 4 to 5 lemons)

1½ teaspoons gelatin

1 cup lemon marmalade

6 large eggs, separated

1½ cups sugar

2 cups heavy cream

For the cake

*Baking spray with flour or unsalted butter and
    all-purpose flour for the pan*

1 Basic Cake Recipe (page 12)

Start the filling: Combine the lemon zest, juice, and gelatin in a medium bowl set over a pot of barely simmering water. Heat until the gelatin is dissolved and the lemon juice is hot. Remove from the heat and refrigerate until the mixture has thickened and begun to jell, about 1 hour. Prepare the cake while it is chilling.

Preheat the oven to 350°F and position a rack in the center. Grease the bottom of an 11 by 17-inch jelly-roll pan, line with parchment paper or aluminum foil, and grease and flour the paper.

Prepare the cake batter according to the recipe.

Pour the batter into the prepared pan, taking care to spread it into all corners of the pan with a rubber spatula. Bake for 15 to 20 minutes, until the surface springs back when poked with your finger and a toothpick inserted in the center of the cake comes out clean. Set the pan on a rack to cool.

When the cake is cool, run a knife around the edge of the pan and turn the cake out onto a cutting board. Remove the parchment paper or foil. Trim ¼ inch from each side of the cake (the edges tend to be dry).

Cut the cake lengthwise into 4 equal strips. Spread ¼ cup of the marmalade on one of the strips. Top with another cake strip and another ¼ cup marmalade. Repeat with the remaining cake and marmalade, ending with a layer of marmalade. Cut the cake into ½-inch-wide slices. Lining them up a few at a time, trim slices to 1½ inches long (see top illustration).

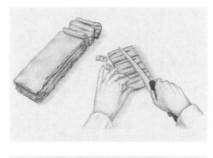

Arrange the slices around the side of a 9-inch spring-form pan, pressing them up against each other (the jam will help make them stick to each other) so that the layers run vertically and will be visible when the cake is unmolded (see bottom illustration). You will have some cake left over for snacking. Set aside while you finish the filling.

Whip the egg yolks and ¾ cup of the sugar in a large bowl with an electric mixer on high speed until thickened and pale yellow, 3 to 4 minutes. Add to the lemon-gelatin mixture and stir until combined.

In another bowl, whip the heavy cream on high speed to soft peaks (see page 7), about 1 minute. With a rubber spatula, fold half the whipped cream into the lemon mixture. Repeat with the remaining cream.

Wash and thoroughly dry the mixing bowl. Whip the egg whites and the remaining ¾ cup sugar on high speed to soft peaks, about 1 minute. Gently fold the egg whites into the lemon mixture until completely smooth and free of streaks.

Pour into the prepared pan; the mixture will come right up to the rim. Freeze until set, at least 6 hours, or overnight.

To unmold, run a knife around the perimeter of the pan, then remove the springform ring. Use a large spatula to transfer the cake to a chilled serving plate. Serve immediately.

Jelly Roll

Almost any kind of jam will work with this recipe, as will Lemon or Lime Curd (page 185). **Serves 8**

For the cake

Baking spray with flour or unsalted butter and
*   all-purpose flour for the pan*

1 Basic Cake Recipe (page 12)

¼ cup confectioners' sugar

For the filling

1 cup fruit jam, stirred in a bowl to soften

Confectioners' sugar

Preheat the oven to 350°F and position a rack in the center. Grease the bottom of an 11 by 17-inch jelly-roll pan, line with parchment paper or aluminum foil, and grease and flour the paper.

Prepare the cake batter according to the recipe. Pour the batter into the prepared pan, taking care to spread it into all corners of the pan with a rubber spatula. Bake for 15 to 20 minutes, until the surface springs back when poked with your finger and a toothpick inserted in the center of the cake comes out clean.

Dust a clean dish towel with the ¼ cup confectioners' sugar and place on a cooling rack. Run a knife around the edge of the pan and immediately turn the cake out onto the sugar-dusted dish towel. Let cool.

When the cake is cool, slide it, on the dish towel, onto the countertop and remove the parchment paper or foil. Trim ¼ inch from each side of the cake (the edges tend to be dry).

Arrange the cake so that a long side is directly in front of you. Spread the jam in an even layer over the cake, going right up to the edges on the long side directly in front of you and the two short sides but only to within 1 inch of the top. Gently roll up the cake from the long side near you, using the dish towel to lift the cake and your fingers to tuck the edge (see the illustration on page 8) and ending with the seam side down. Use the dish towel to help press the cake into an even roll. Remove the dish towel and transfer the roll to a serving platter. Serve immediately or refrigerate until ready to serve. Just before serving, sprinkle the jelly roll with confectioners' sugar.

Lemon Coconut Roulade

This light and lemony dessert is perfect on a hot summer night after a day at the beach. Lemon and coconut are a popular Southern pairing, and the rum-scented Whipped Cream adds a Caribbean influence. **Serves 8 to 10**

For the filling

1 recipe Lemon Curd (page 185)

For the cake

*Baking spray with flour or unsalted butter and
  all-purpose flour for the pan*

2 cups sweetened shredded coconut

1 Basic Cake Recipe (page 12)

For the frosting

½ recipe Whipped Cream (page 197), flavored with rum

Prepare the Lemon Curd and place it in the refrigerator to set.

Preheat the oven to 350°F and position a rack in the center. Grease the bottom of an 11 by 17-inch jelly-roll pan, line with parchment paper or aluminum foil, and grease and flour the paper.

Spread the coconut on a baking sheet and toast for 8 to 10 minutes, until lightly browned, with some white spots. Let cool.

Grind 1½ cups of the coconut in a food processor until fine, about 30 seconds.

Prepare the cake batter according to the recipe, with the following change: In Step 1, add the ground coconut to the flour mixture.

Pour the batter into the prepared pan, taking care to spread it into all corners of the pan with a rubber spatula. Bake for 15 to 20 minutes, until the surface springs back when poked with your finger and a toothpick inserted in the center of the cake comes out clean.

Run a knife around the edge of the pan and immediately turn the cake out onto a rack covered with a clean dish towel to cool.

When the cake is cool, slide it, on the dish towel, onto the countertop and remove the parchment paper or foil. Trim ¼ inch from each side of the cake (the edges tend to be dry).

Arrange the cake so that a long side is directly in front of you. Spread the lemon curd in an even layer over the cake, going right up to the edges on the long side directly in front of you and the two short sides but only to within 1 inch of the top. Gently roll up the cake from the long side near you, using the dish towel to lift the cake and your fingers to tuck in the edges (see the illustration on page 8) and ending with the seam side down. Use the dish towel to help press the cake into an even roll. Remove the dish towel and transfer the roulade to a serving platter. Cover and refrigerate for at least 30 minutes, or for up to 48 hours.

Prepare the whipped cream. Spread the whipped cream in an even layer all over the roulade. Sprinkle with the reserved coconut. Serve immediately.

Orange Vanilla Baked Alaska

Baking ice cream and cake isn't as crazy as it seems—the Chinese have been doing it for hundreds of years. The French supposedly learned it from the Chinese, and we, of course, learned it from them. The only drawback to this dessert? You have to serve it right away, as the meringue coating won't hold up well in the freezer and the ice cream won't last long out of the freezer. **Serves 8 to 10**

For the cake

*Baking spray with flour or unsalted butter and
    all-purpose flour for the pan*

1 Basic Cake Recipe (page 12)

½ cup orange marmalade

For the filling and topping

1 cup orange marmalade

*1 recipe Vanilla Ice Cream (page 184) or ½ gallon store-bought
    vanilla ice cream, softened*

5 large egg whites

⅔ cup sugar

Preheat the oven to 350°F and position a rack in the center. Grease the bottom of an 11 by 17-inch jelly-roll pan, line with parchment paper or aluminum foil, and grease and flour the paper.

Prepare the cake batter according to the recipe, with the following change: In Step 2, add the ½ cup of marmalade to the warm milk and butter and stir until completely melted.

Pour the batter into the prepared pan, taking care to spread it into all corners of the pan with a rubber spatula. Bake for 15 to 20 minutes, until the surface springs back when poked with your finger and a toothpick inserted in the center of the cake comes out clean. Set the cake on a rack to cool.

Line a 9 by 5-inch loaf pan with plastic wrap, leaving plenty of overhang on the sides. (When the cake is finished, you will use the plastic wrap to remove the cake from the pan.)

When the cake is cool, run a knife around the edge of the pan and turn the cake out onto a cutting board. Remove the parchment or foil. Trim ¼ inch from each side of the cake (the edges tend to be dry). Using your loaf pan as a stencil, cut out a piece of cake that will just fit in the bottom of the loaf pan. Again using your loaf pan as a guide, cut out a piece that will fit just inside the top of the pan (once it is filled). Then cut out pieces that will fit along the four sides of the pan. Once the pieces are all cut, line the pan with the cake; you may have to trim them as you lay them in the pan. Set the top piece aside.

Combine the cup of marmalade and the ice cream in a bowl, stirring until well blended. Pour the ice cream into the prepared pan and top with the remaining piece of cake. Pull the plastic wrap over the top to cover. Freeze until set, at least 1 hour, or up to 1 week.

Once the cake is set, prepare the meringue: Beat the egg whites in a large bowl with an electric mixer at medium speed until frothy, about 1 minute. Slowly add the sugar, then increase the speed to high and whip to stiff peaks (see page 7).

Preheat the oven to 400°F and position a rack in the center.

To unmold the cake, peel back the plastic wrap, place an ovenproof plate or baking sheet over the pan, and invert the cake onto the plate. Pull down on the plastic wrap as you lift up the cake pan and remove it. Gently remove the plastic wrap.

Using a metal icing spatula, spread the meringue thickly and evenly over the cake. Using the tip of the spatula, pull up small peaks of meringue all over the top and sides of the cake. Bake the cake until the meringue is set and evenly browned, 6 to 8 minutes. Serve immediately.

Ring Ding Roulade

This is a taste of childhood, reminiscent of Drake's cream-filled chocolate snack cakes but so much better. It's pure simplicity, moist chocolate cake and sweet whipped cream topped with a crispy chocolate coating. Perfect for birthday parties. The glaze will lose its luster when refrigerated, so don't glaze the bombe until about 30 minutes before you're ready to serve it. Do refrigerate leftovers; the glaze will have a matte rather than shiny finish. **Serves 8 to 10**

For the cake

Baking spray with flour or unsalted butter and all-purpose flour for the pan

1 Basic Cake Recipe (page 12)

4 ounces semisweet chocolate, chopped

For the filling and frosting

1 recipe Whipped Cream (page 197)

1 recipe Chocolate Glaze (page 194)

Preheat the oven to 350°F and position a rack in the center. Grease the bottom of an 11 by 17-inch jelly-roll pan, line with parchment paper or aluminum foil, and grease and flour the paper.

Prepare the cake batter according to the recipe, with the following change: In Step 5, melt the chocolate in a large bowl in the microwave, or melt the chocolate in a double boiler and then transfer it to a large bowl (this must be done at the last minute so the chocolate doesn't set). Add the warm milk and butter to the chocolate and stir until combined, then add the chocolate to half of the batter. Stir quickly but gently until the chocolate is evenly distributed. Gently fold the chocolate batter into the remaining batter until completely combined and no streaks remain.

Pour the batter into the prepared pan, taking care to spread it into all corners of the pan with a rubber spatula. Bake for 15 to 20 minutes, until the surface springs back when poked with your finger and a toothpick inserted in the center of the cake comes out with a few moist crumbs but is not wet.

Run a knife around the edge of the pan and immediately turn the cake out onto a rack covered with a clean dish towel to cool.

While the cake is cooling, prepare the whipped cream. Cover and refrigerate.

When the cake is cool, slide it, on the dish towel, onto the countertop and remove the parchment paper or foil. Trim ¼ inch from each side of the cake (the edges tend to be dry).

Arrange the cake so that a long side is directly in front of you. Spread the whipped cream in an even layer over the cake, going right up to the edges on the long side directly in front of you and the two short sides but only to within 1 inch of the top. Gently roll up the cake from the long side near you, using the dish towel to lift the cake and your fingers to tuck in the edge (see the illustration on page 8) and ending with the seam side down. Use the dish towel to help press the cake into an even roll. Remove the dish towel and transfer the roulade to a platter. Refrigerate for at least 30 minutes or up to 48 hours.

Prepare the chocolate glaze just before you are ready to use it. Transfer the roulade to a wire rack set over a baking sheet. Pour the glaze over the roulade, starting at one end and running the entire length, reserving a bit in the bowl for any touch-ups. Using an offset spatula, spread the glaze in an even layer over the entire cake, tucking in some glaze on the underside as well. Let stand at room temperature until set, about 30 minutes.

Use a large spatula to transfer the roulade to a serving plate. Serve immediately.

Root Beer Float Ice Cream Cake

Greg's favorite summer memory is of childhood visits to Jumpin' Jack under the bridge along the Mohawk River in Schenectady, where he always got the fried clams and a root beer float. While pastry chef at Hamersley's in Boston, he re-created that memory with homemade sarsparilla ice cream. Since sarsparilla bark is hard for the average home cook to find, Greg approximates the flavor here with root beer candy. You can garnish the cake with whole root beer barrels, but we prefer to put a few in a plastic bag and whack them with a rolling pin so they break into pieces and are easier to eat. **Serves 8 to 10**

For the cake

Baking spray with flour or unsalted butter and all-purpose flour for the pans

1 Basic Cake Recipe (page 12)

10 root beer barrel candies, finely ground (about ¼ cup)

For the filling and frosting

1 recipe Vanilla Ice Cream (page 184) or ½ gallon store-bought vanilla ice cream, softened

20 root beer barrel candies, finely ground (about ½ cup)

¼ cup Simple Syrup (page 198)

1 recipe White Mountain Frosting (page 192)

1 tablespoon vanilla extract

Crushed root beer barrel candy for garnish

Preheat the oven to 350°F and position a rack in the center. Grease and flour two 9-inch round cake pans.

Prepare the cake batter according to the recipe, with the following change: In Step 1, add the ground root beer barrels to the flour mixture.

Divide the batter between the prepared pans. Bake for 15 to 20 minutes, until the edges pull back from the pan and a toothpick inserted in the center of the cake comes out clean. Cool the cakes in the pans on a rack.

When the cakes are cool, run a knife around the edge of each pan and turn them out onto the rack.

Combine the ice cream and the ½ cup ground root beer candy.

Line a 9-inch round cake pan with plastic wrap, leaving plenty of overhang on the sides. (When the cake is finished, you will use the plastic wrap to remove the cake from the pan.) Place one cake layer in the pan, right side up. Brush the top of the cake with about 2 tablespoons simple syrup. Pour the ice cream over the cake, spreading it in an even layer. Brush the remaining simple syrup on the top of the second cake layer and place it, upside down, on top of the ice cream. Press down gently. Pull the plastic wrap over the top to cover, and place another 9-inch cake pan on top of the cake to weight it. Freeze until set, at least 4 hours, or up to 48 hours.

When the cake has set completely, prepare the frosting, adding the additional tablespoon of vanilla.

To unmold the cake, peel back the plastic wrap, place a plate over the pan, and invert the cake onto the plate. Pull down on the plastic wrap as you lift up the cake pan and remove it. Gently remove the plastic wrap.

Frost the cake with the frosting (see page 9 for step-by-step illustrations). Garnish with crushed root beer barrels.

Serve immediately, or hold in the freezer for up to 2 hours.

Spiced Pumpkin Mousse Charlotte

Pumpkin desserts can be heavy. Here the mousse is light, not as dense as pumpkin pie sometimes is. The warm spiced gingerbread highlights the pumpkin flavor. You will need to bake two sheets of cake for this recipe. If you don't have two jelly-roll pans, just make one recipe of batter at a time. **Serves 8 to 10**

For the cakes

*Baking spray with flour or unsalted butter and
all-purpose flour for the pans*

*2 Basic Cake Recipes (page 12), with only
1 cup granulated sugar total*

1 tablespoon plus 1 teaspoon ground ginger

1 teaspoon ground cinnamon

½ teaspoon ground allspice

½ cup unsulphured (mild) molasses

1 cup packed dark brown sugar

For the filling

1 packet (2 ½ teaspoons) gelatin

1 cup milk

2 cups canned pumpkin puree

2 large egg yolks

¼ cup packed dark brown sugar

⅓ cup granulated sugar

Pinch of salt

1 teaspoon ground cinnamon

½ teaspoon ground allspice

1 teaspoon ground ginger

1 cup heavy cream

Preheat the oven to 350°F and position the racks in the upper and lower center. Grease the bottom of two 11 by 17-inch jelly-roll pans, line them with parchment paper or aluminum foil, and grease and flour the paper.

Prepare the double batch of cake batter according to the recipe, with the following changes: In Step 1, add the ginger, cinnamon, and allspice to the flour mixture. In Step 2, add the molasses to the warm milk and butter and stir to dissolve. In Step 3, replace half of the granulated sugar with the dark brown sugar, using 1 cup granulated sugar for the double batch.

Pour the batter into the prepared pans, taking care to spread it into all corners of the pans with a rubber spatula. Bake for 15 to 20 minutes, until the surface springs back when poked with your finger and a toothpick inserted in the center of the cakes comes out clean. Set the cakes on racks to cool.

Prepare the filling: Sprinkle the gelatin over the milk and set aside to soften.

Combine the pumpkin, egg yolks, brown sugar, granulated sugar, salt, and spices in a medium saucepan over medium heat and cook until hot, 3 to 5 minutes; do not boil. Add the milk, stirring to combine, and then bring to a boil, stirring. Cook, stirring constantly, for 2 minutes (to cook the eggs). Transfer to a large bowl and refrigerate until cool.

When the cakes are cool, run a knife around the edges of the pans and turn the cakes out onto a large cutting board. Remove the parchment paper or foil. Trim ¼ inch from each side of the cakes (the edges tend to be dry). Cut out two 8-inch disks from one cake. Cut out a 10-inch disk from the other cake, and then cut the rest of the cake into 3-inch-wide strips.

Grease a 9-inch springform pan and lay both 8-inch circles in the bottom (because the filling is wet, the bottom needs to be reinforced). Cut the 3-inch strips crosswise into 2½-inch pieces and arrange them around the side of the pan, overlapping them slightly (you will need about 17 pieces).

When the pumpkin mixture is cool, whip the heavy cream on high speed to soft peaks (see page 7), about 1 minute. Add half the cream to the pumpkin and fold gently until just combined. Add the remaining cream and fold until completely combined and no streaks remain.

Pour the mousse into the prepared pan. Cut the 10-inch disk of cake into 12 equal wedges. Place the wedges on top of the filling, overlapping them slightly (see the illustration on page 113). Refrigerate until set, at least 6 hours, or overnight.

When ready to serve, remove the springform. Using a large spatula (or two), transfer the cake to a serving platter. Serve with Whipped Cream (page 197).

Strawberry Bombe

Greg first created this cake more than twenty years ago for a friend's birthday party. The beautiful presentation—the bright white exterior and the impressive layers within—makes it a sophisticated dessert for special occasions. The sour cream tames the sweetness of the filling so the cake isn't at all cloying. **Serves 10 to 12**

For the cake

*Baking spray with flour or unsalted butter and
all-purpose flour for the pan*

1 Basic Cake Recipe (page 12)

For the filling and topping

1 cup heavy cream

2 tablespoons sour cream

2 tablespoons sugar

½ teaspoon vanilla extract

¼ cup framboise or raspberry- or strawberry-flavored eau de vie

3 cups hulled and quartered strawberries (about 3 pints)

3 tablespoons Simple Syrup (page 198)

½ recipe Whipped Cream (page 197)

Strawberries for garnish (optional)

Preheat the oven to 350°F and position a rack in the center. Grease the bottom of an 11 by 17-inch jelly-roll pan, line with parchment paper or aluminum foil, and grease and flour the paper.

Prepare the cake batter according to the recipe.

Pour the batter into the prepared pan, taking care to spread it into all corners of the pan with a rubber spatula. Bake for 15 to 20 minutes, until the surface springs back when poked with your finger and a toothpick inserted in the center of the cake comes out clean. Set the cake on a rack to cool.

Line a 1½-quart bowl (we like Pyrex) with plastic wrap, leaving plenty of overhang on the sides. (When the cake is finished, you will use the plastic wrap to remove the cake from the pan.)

When the cake is cool, run a knife around the edge of the pan and turn the cake out onto a large cutting board. Remove the parchment paper or foil. Trim ¼ inch from each side of the cake (the edges tend to be dry). Cut the cake into pieces according to the diagram on page 8. Line the bowl with the cake according to the illustrations on page 8, trimming any excess that comes above the rim of the bowl and reserving the extra pieces and trimmings.

Prepare the filling: With a mixer on high speed, whip together the heavy cream and sour cream in a large bowl until slightly thickened, about 1 minute. Add the sugar, vanilla, and 1 tablespoon of the framboise, and continue to whip to soft peaks (see page 7), about 2 minutes longer. Using a rubber spatula, gently fold in the strawberries until evenly distributed.

Combine the simple syrup and the remaining 3 tablespoons framboise. Brush the cake in the bowl liberally with the syrup. Fill the bowl with two-thirds of the strawberry filling, pushing it down in the center and spreading it up the sides of the bowl. Top with the reserved pieces of cake and press down gently to form an even layer with no pieces overlapping. Trim as necessary. Brush the cake liberally with the syrup. Add the remaining filling. Brush the disk of cake with the syrup and place it, syrup side down, on top of the filling. Pull the plastic wrap over the top to cover. Top with a plate slightly smaller than the bowl and set a 1-pound weight (like a block of butter) on it. Refrigerate until set, at least 2 hours, or up to 24 hours.

Prepare the whipped cream.

Turn out the bombe just before serving: Peel back the plastic wrap from the cake and then turn the cake out onto a serving plate; you may have to pull slightly on the plastic wrap to get the bowl off. Gently remove the plastic wrap and discard.

Frost the bombe with the whipped cream. Garnish with strawberries, if desired. Serve immediately.

Summer Berry Pudding

Summer puddings were originally served in mid-nineteenth-century England to the sick and elderly as a healthful alternative to heavy custards. Though these puddings are traditionally made by lining a bowl with slices of white bread and filling the bowl with fresh fruit, we find that our sponge cake works just as well at absorbing the sweet berry juices and turning a deep purple color. Use the freshest, ripest local berries you can find. **Serves 8 to 10**

For the cake

*Baking spray with flour or unsalted butter and
    all-purpose flour for the pan*

1 Basic Cake Recipe (page 12)

For the filling

1 packet (2½ teaspoons) gelatin

¼ cup fresh lemon juice

1 cup sugar

*6 cups mixed berries, such as sliced strawberries, blueberries,
    and blackberries*

Confectioners' sugar

Preheat the oven to 350°F and position a rack in the center. Grease the bottom of an 11 by 17-inch jelly-roll pan, line with parchment paper or aluminum foil, and grease and flour the paper.

Prepare the cake batter according to the recipe.

Pour the batter into the prepared pan, taking care to spread it into all corners of the pan with a rubber spatula. Bake for 15 to 20 minutes, until the surface springs back when poked with your finger and a toothpick inserted in the center of the cake comes out clean. Set the cake on a rack to cool.

Line a 1½-quart bowl (we like Pyrex) with plastic wrap, leaving plenty of overhang on the sides. (When the cake is finished, you will use the plastic wrap to remove the cake from the pan.)

When the cake is cool, run a knife around the edge of the pan and turn the cake out onto a large cutting board. Remove the parchment paper or foil. Trim ¼ inch from each side of the cake (the edges tend to be dry). Cut the cake into pieces according to the diagram on page 8. Line the bowl with the cake according to the illustrations on page 8, trimming any excess that comes above the rim of the bowl.

Prepare the filling: Sprinkle the gelatin over the lemon juice in a medium saucepan and set aside for 1 minute to soften. Add the sugar and heat over medium heat just until hot, about 1 minute, stirring to dissolve the gelatin. Add the berries and bring to a boil. Cook for 1 minute longer.

Pour the warm berry mixture into the prepared bowl. Top with the reserved cake disk. Pull the plastic wrap over the top to cover. Top with a plate slightly smaller than the bowl and set a 1-pound weight (like a block of butter) on top. Refrigerate until set, at least 2 hours, or up to 48 hours.

Turn out the pudding just before serving: Peel back the plastic wrap from the cake and turn the cake out onto a serving plate; you may have to pull slightly on the plastic wrap to get the bowl off. Gently remove the plastic wrap and discard.

Sprinkle with confectioners' sugar and serve (if you sprinkle it on too soon, it will just dissolve into the cake).

Trifle

Trifle—sherry-soaked sponge cake layered with cream and fruit—dates back to mid-eighteenth-century England. Trifle is a great way to use up leftover pieces of stale cake, which better absorbs the sherry. Be sure to use a glass bowl for trifle, so you can see the layers of cake, fruit, custard, and jam. Feel free to play around a little bit with the recipe, varying the liqueur and substituting one fruit for another. **Serves 8 to 10**

For the cake

*Baking spray with flour or unsalted butter and
    all-purpose flour for the pan*

1 Basic Cake Recipe (page 12)

¼ cup all-purpose flour

For assembly

½ cup dry sherry

2 cups Pastry Cream (page 187)

*2 cups mixed soft fruit, such as berries, sliced kiwi, peaches,
    or pineapple, or cooked apples and pears*

1 cup fruit jam, stirred vigorously to break up any larger pieces

1 recipe Whipped Cream (page 197)

Berries for garnish

Preheat the oven to 350°F and position a rack in the center. Grease the bottom of an 11 by 17-inch jelly-roll pan, line with parchment paper or aluminum foil, and grease and flour the paper.

Prepare the cake batter according to the recipe, with the following change: In Step 1, add the additional ¼ cup flour to the flour mixture (1 cup total).

Pour the batter into the prepared pan, taking care to spread it into all corners of the pan with a rubber spatula. Bake for 15 to 20 minutes, until the surface springs back when poked with your finger and a toothpick inserted in the center of the cake comes out clean.

When the cake is cool, cut it into 1-inch pieces. Spread out on a cookie sheet and allow to air-dry while you prepare the pastry cream.

Assemble the trifle: Place one-third of the cake pieces in the bottom of a large decorative glass bowl (about 6-cup capacity). Sprinkle 3 tablespoons of the sherry over the cake. Top with ¾ cup of the pastry cream and spread the pastry cream evenly over the cake, taking care to push the cream in between the pieces of cake and right up to the edges of the bowl. Scatter half of the fruit on top of the cream, and drop spoonfuls of half of the jam over the fruit, especially at the sides of the bowl (this makes for a nicer presentation). Top with half of the remaining cake, the remaining 3 tablespoons sherry, ¾ cup pastry cream, the remaining cup of fruit, and the remaining ½ cup jam. Spread the remaining cake pieces on top and sprinkle with the remaining 2 tablespoons sherry. Press down gently with your hand. Spread the remaining pastry cream over the top of the cake. Cover with plastic wrap and refrigerate until set, at least 1 hour, or up to 24 hours.

Just before serving, prepare the whipped cream. Spread the cream in an even layer on top of the trifle, and garnish with berries.

Layer Cakes

When you need a party cake—for your daughter's birthday, your niece's graduation, Grandma's retirement—what do you make? A layer cake, of course. The ultimate party cake is a standard on celebratory occasions—who doesn't have a photograph of their children at their first birthday party, with a big smile covered in frosting?

You know what to expect with these desserts: cake, filling, and frosting. But that doesn't mean you want the expected. How about bananas and peanut butter in Elvis's Favorite Cake? How about Margarita Cake for your son's twenty-first birthday, Snickers Cake for Mother's Day, or Strawberry Mousse Cake for Valentine's Day?

You can make the cake layers ahead of time and freeze them. Wrapped well in plastic, they will keep for up to 1 month. Unwrap and thaw at room temperature for about an hour. Or bake the layers and store, covered, at room temperature for up to 2 days. If you do make the cakes ahead of time, the tops will "bloom," meaning a moist sugar layer will appear on the top of the cake. Just scrape it off with a knife; it will come off quite easily.

Some of these cakes need to set up in the refrigerator for a few hours, so, as always, be sure to read the recipe through before you begin.

A final word on presentation: frosting a cake is not difficult, but it may take a while to get the hang of it. Actually, we prefer the rustic homemade look of a frosted cake a lot more than the overly finished, polished look found in some bakeshops. To that end we have included detailed instructions and illustrations on frosting a cake simply and easily. And if your cake doesn't look perfect, you can always cover the sides with cookie crumbs, nuts, or sprinkles.

Apricot Ginger Cake

This European-style cake has a simple jam filling instead of a creamy American-style filling. There's plenty of richness in this cake, thanks to the buttercream frosting. **Serves 10 to 12**

For the cake

Baking spray with flour or unsalted butter and all-purpose flour for the pans

1 Basic Cake Recipe (page 12)

1 teaspoon ground ginger

For the filling and frosting

1 recipe Buttercream (page 190)

¼ cup chopped candied ginger

1 teaspoon ground ginger

1 cup apricot jam

Preheat the oven to 350°F and position a rack in the center. Grease and flour two 9-inch round cake pans.

Prepare the cake batter according to the recipe, with the following change: In Step 1, add the ground ginger to the flour mixture.

Divide the batter between the prepared pans. Bake for 15 to 20 minutes, until the edges pull back from the pans and a toothpick inserted in the center of the cakes comes out clean. Cool the cakes in the pan on a rack. When the cakes are cool, run a knife around the edges of the pans and turn them out onto the rack.

Prepare the buttercream. Add the candied ginger and ground ginger and mix on high speed until fully combined. Set aside.

Place one of the layers on a cake stand or plate. Spread the jam in an even layer on the cake. Place the second cake upside down on top of the jam. Frost the cake with the buttercream (see page 9 for step-by-step illustrations). Chill for at least 1 hour, or up to 48 hours, before serving.

Black Forest Cake

Known as *Schwarzwalder Kirschtorte* in its native Germany, Black Forest Cherry Torte is an American classic as well. The Black Forest region is known for its sour cherries and the liquor made from those cherries: kirsch. The unique flavor of this chocolate cake comes from the cherries. **Serves 10 to 12**

For the cake

*Baking spray with flour or unsalted butter and
    all-purpose flour for the pans*

1 Basic Cake Recipe (page 12)

4 ounces semisweet chocolate, chopped

For the filling

5 tablespoons Simple Syrup (page 198)

1 tablespoon kirsch or other cherry-flavored liqueur or brandy

12 ounces frozen cherries, defrosted

2 tablespoons brandy

1½ teaspoons gelatin

1½ cups heavy cream

3 tablespoons granulated sugar

Confectioners' sugar

Preheat the oven to 350°F and position a rack in the center. Grease and flour two 9-inch cake pans.

Prepare the cake batter according to the recipe, with the following change: In Step 5, melt the chocolate in a large bowl in the microwave, or melt the chocolate in a double boiler and then transfer it to a large bowl (this must be done at the last minute so the chocolate doesn't set). Add the warm milk and butter to the chocolate and stir until combined, then add the chocolate to half of the batter. Stir quickly but gently until the chocolate is evenly distributed.

Gently fold the chocolate batter into the remaining batter until completely combined and no streaks remain.

Divide the batter between the prepared pans. Bake for 15 to 20 minutes, until the edges pull back from the pans and a toothpick inserted in the center of the cakes comes out clean. Cool the cakes in the pan on a rack.

When the cakes are cool, run a knife around the edges of the pans and turn them out onto the rack.

Line a 9-inch cake pan with plastic wrap, leaving plenty of overhang on the sides. (When the cake is finished, you will use the plastic wrap to remove the cake from the pan.) Place one cake layer in the pan, right side up. Combine the simple syrup and kirsch and brush the top of the cake with about 3 tablespoons syrup. Brush the top of the remaining cake layer with the remaining simple syrup, and set aside while you prepare the filling.

Pour the cherries into a strainer set over a bowl. Sprinkle the cherries with the brandy. Press gently with a spoon to release as much juice as possible. Place 3 tablespoons of the cherry liquid in a small pot and sprinkle with the gelatin (you can discard any remaining cherry juice). Let stand for 2 minutes off the heat to soften, then warm over medium heat and stir until the gelatin is melted. Slowly add ¼ cup of the heavy cream and stir until combined. Add the remaining 1¼ cups cream and stir until combined. Transfer to the bowl of a stand mixer fitted with a whisk, or use a hand mixer, and add the granulated sugar. Mix on high speed to soft peaks (see page 7), about 1 minute.

Spread half of the cream in an even layer over the cake in the prepared pan. Arrange the cherries in the cream, making a ring right at the edge around the entire circumference of the pan (these will show when you serve the cake) and scattering the rest across the cream. Top the cherries with the remaining cream, spreading it in an even layer. Place the second cake layer upside down on top of the cream and press down gently. Pull the plastic wrap over the top to cover. Place another 9-inch cake pan on top of the cake and place a 1-pound weight (such as a pound of butter) in the pan. Refrigerate until set, at least 4 hours, or up to 48 hours.

To unmold the cake, peel back the plastic wrap, place a plate over the pan, and invert the cake onto the plate. Pull down on the plastic wrap as you lift up the cake pan and remove it.

When ready to serve, gently remove the plastic wrap and sprinkle the cake with confectioners' sugar.

Boston Cream Pie

Seeing as this is the official state dessert of our home state of Massachusetts, we had to include a recipe. It's technically a cake, not a pie—it seems the line dividing the two was quite thin back in the nineteenth century—and it has been a classic for more than one hundred years. The Parker House Hotel in Boston takes credit for the invention of this dessert, claiming to have served it since 1856. We love the rustic nature of this cake; it's okay if it looks a little sloppy with the custard oozing out between the layers. **Serves 8 to 10**

For the filling

1 recipe Pastry Cream (page 187)

For the cake

Baking spray with flour or unsalted butter and all-purpose flour for the pans

1 Basic Cake Recipe (page 12)

For the frosting

¼ cup Simple Syrup (page 198)

1 recipe Chocolate Glaze (page 194)

Prepare the pastry cream and place it in the refrigerator to set.

Preheat the oven to 350°F and position a rack in the center. Grease and flour two 9-inch round cake pans.

Prepare the cake batter according to the recipe.

Divide the batter between the prepared pans. Bake for 15 to 20 minutes, until the edges pull away from the pans and a toothpick inserted in the center of the cakes comes out clean. Cool the cakes in the pans on a rack.

When the cakes are cool, run a knife around the edges of the pans and turn them out onto the rack. Brush the top of each layer with 2 tablespoons simple syrup.

Prepare the glaze. Turn one of the layers upside down and place it on a wire rack set over a baking sheet or large plate. Pour all of the glaze into the center of the cake. Using an offset spatula, spread the glaze evenly over the top of the cake and down the sides, making sure that the sides are evenly covered. Let set for 20 minutes before assembling the cake (don't put it in the refrigerator, because that will make the shiny glaze dull).

Place the remaining cake layer (the unglazed one) on a cake stand or plate, right side up. Stir the pastry cream a few times to smooth it. Spread the pastry cream evenly over the cake, right to the edges. Place the glazed cake layer on top of the pastry cream, pressing down slightly so that some of the pastry cream oozes out the sides. Serve immediately.

Cappuccino Cake

Coffee and dessert in one great cake? This is our playful take on a cappuccino, with a coffee-flavored cake and buttercream, a vanilla "foam" topping, and a final dusting of cinnamon. No cappuccino machine required. **Serves 10 to 12**

For the cake

Baking spray with flour or unsalted butter and
all-purpose flour for the pans

1 Basic Cake Recipe (page 12)

½ teaspoon ground cinnamon

1 tablespoon instant coffee

For the filling and frosting

1 recipe Buttercream (page 190)

2 tablespoons instant coffee

1 tablespoon dark rum or water

¼ cup Simple Syrup (page 198)

¼ teaspoon ground cinnamon

Preheat the oven to 350°F and position a rack in the center. Grease and flour two 9-inch round cake pans.

Prepare the cake batter according to the recipe, with the following changes: In Step 1, add the cinnamon to the flour mixture. In Step 2, stir the coffee into the warm milk and butter until dissolved.

Divide the batter between the prepared pans. Bake for 15 to 20 minutes, until the edges pull back from the pans and a toothpick inserted in the center of the cakes comes out clean. Cool the cakes in the pans on a rack.

When the cakes are cool, run a knife around the edges of the pans and turn them out onto the rack.

Prepare the buttercream. Set aside one-third of the buttercream (this will be the "foam" topping on the cake). Dissolve the coffee in the rum. Add the coffee mixture to the remaining buttercream and mix on high speed until fully combined.

Place one of the layers on a cake stand or plate. Use a pastry brush to lightly moisten the top of the layer with about 2 tablespoons of the simple syrup. Spread about half of the coffee buttercream in an even layer on the cake, leaving a ⅛-inch border all around the edge (the buttercream will spread when you put the second layer on top). Moisten the top of the remaining cake layer with the remaining simple syrup. Place the second cake upside down on top of the buttercream.

Frost the top of the cake with the plain buttercream. Frost the sides with the remaining coffee buttercream. Sprinkle the cinnamon over the top of the cake.

Chill for at least 1 hour, up to 48 hours, before serving.

Caramel Cake

A traditional American frosting from a bygone era, caramel frosting is a quintessentially Southern delight. It is not nearly as rich as buttercream, but it is much sweeter. It's so sweet, in fact, that it works best with just one layer of cake. Don't be put off by the idea of making caramel. It isn't as difficult as people think it is—but do take care, as the caramel gets very hot. **Serves 10 to 12**

For the cake

*Baking spray with flour or unsalted butter and
    all-purpose flour for the pan*

1 Basic Cake Recipe (page 12)

For the frosting

1 recipe Caramel Frosting (page 193)

Preheat the oven to 350°F and position a rack in the center. Grease and flour a 9 by 13-inch baking pan.

Prepare the cake batter according to the recipe.

Pour the batter into the prepared pan. Bake for 25 to 30 minutes, until the edges pull back from the pan and a toothpick inserted in the center of the cake comes out clean. Cool the cake in the pan on a rack.

When the cake is cool, run a knife around the edge of the pan and turn the cake out onto a cake plate.

Prepare the frosting. Frost the cake with the frosting (you will have a thin layer of frosting, which is fine, because the frosting is so sweet).

Chill for at least 1 hour, or up to 48 hours, before serving.

Carrot Cake

This is Keri's absolute favorite cake; Greg made it for her wedding. The hot milk sponge cake is very tender and moist, and adding carrots makes it even more so. Usually carrot cakes use shredded carrots, but we grind them into smaller pieces, which makes the cake that much moister. Greg's been playing around with the blend of spices for years, adjusting the types and amounts until he found a formula that was well balanced. The blend lends a wintry, spicy flavor to the cake with no one spice dominating. Of course, to some, it's all about the cream cheese frosting. Though it likely won't last the day, carrot cake actually gets better with age as the spices mellow and blend. **Serves 10 to 12**

For the cake

*Baking spray with flour or unsalted butter and
  all-purpose flour for the pans*

8 ounces carrots, sliced into ¼-inch disks

*1 Basic Cake Recipe (page 12), minus the
  vanilla and ½ cup of the granulated sugar*

¼ teaspoon ground nutmeg

1 teaspoon ground cinnamon

½ teaspoon ground allspice

½ cup packed dark brown sugar

½ cup (about 3 ounces) chopped walnuts

For the frosting

1 recipe Cream Cheese Frosting (page 191)

Preheat the oven to 350°F and position a rack in the center. Grease and flour two 9-inch round cake pans.

Grind the carrots in a food processor until very fine, about 20 seconds. You should have about 2 cups ground carrots.

Prepare the cake batter according to the recipe, with the following changes: In Step 1, add the nutmeg, cinnamon, and allspice to the flour mixture. In Step 2, omit the vanilla. In Step 3, replace ½ cup of the granulated sugar with the dark brown sugar. In Step 5, gently fold the carrots and walnuts into the finished batter.

Divide the batter between the prepared pans. Bake for 15 to 20 minutes, until the edges pull back from the pans and a toothpick inserted in the center of the cakes comes out clean. Cool the cakes in the pans on a rack.

When the cakes are cool, run a knife around the edges of the pans and turn the cakes out onto the rack.

Prepare the cream cheese frosting. Place one of the layers on a cake stand or plate. Spread about one-third of the frosting in an even layer on the cake. Place the second layer upside down on the frosting. Frost the cake with the remaining frosting (see page 9 for step-by-step illustrations).

Chill for at least 1 hour, or up to 48 hours, before serving.

Cassata

This traditional Sicilian cannoli cake features thin soft layers of cake surrounding a sweet ricotta filling, lending the dessert an almost puddinglike consistency. To make it even more special, pick up some homemade ricotta at your local Italian market. **Serves 8 to 10**

For the cake

Baking spray with flour or unsalted butter and
  all-purpose flour for the pan

1 Basic Cake Recipe (page 12)

For the filling and frosting

1 pound ricotta

½ cup sugar

½ teaspoon ground cinnamon

1½ teaspoons grated orange zest

1 ounce semisweet chocolate, grated

7 tablespoons Simple Syrup (page 198)

2 tablespoons dark rum

1 recipe Chocolate Buttercream (page 190)

Preheat the oven to 350°F and position a rack in the center. Grease the bottom of an 11 by 17-inch jelly-roll pan, line with parchment paper or aluminum foil, and grease and flour the paper.

Prepare the cake batter according to the recipe.

Pour the batter into the prepared pan, taking care to spread it into all corners of the pan with a rubber spatula. Bake for 15 to 18 minutes, until the surface springs back when poked with your finger and a toothpick inserted in the center of the cake comes out clean. Set the cake on a rack to cool.

While the cake is cooling, prepare the filling: Combine the ricotta, sugar, cinnamon, and orange zest in the bowl of a stand mixer and mix with the whisk at high speed until combined. With a rubber spatula, gently fold in the grated chocolate.

When the cake is cool, run a knife around the edge of the pan and turn the cake out onto a large cutting board. Remove the parchment paper or foil. Trim ¼ inch from each side of the cake (the edges tend to be dry). Cut the cake into quarters: With a long side facing you, make one cut horizontally through the center, and one cut vertically through the center.

Place one piece of the cake on a cake stand or plate. Use a pastry brush to lightly moisten the top of the layer with about 2 tablespoons of the simple syrup. Place one-third of the ricotta filling on top of the cake, and spread it in an even layer. Moisten the top of another cake layer with 1 tablespoon simple syrup. Place the layer moistened side down on top of the ricotta, and then moisten the top with 1 tablespoon syrup. Repeat with the remaining filling and cake, ending with a cake layer brushed only on the bottom with syrup. Refrigerate while you prepare the buttercream.

Frost the cake with the chocolate buttercream (see page 9 for step-by-step illustrations).

Chill for at least 1 hour, or up to 48 hours, before serving.

Coconut Cream Cake

Coconut cake and coconut cream pie are two great desserts, so why not combine them into one great cake? You might think that fresh coconuts would give you the best coconut flavor, but the work required is difficult and time-consuming and, frankly, not worth the effort. Canned coconut milk and shredded coconut are just as good and make this cake much easier to prepare. **Serves 10 to 12**

For the filling
1 recipe Coconut Pastry Cream (page 187)

For the cake
Baking spray with flour or unsalted butter and
*   all-purpose flour for the pans*

1½ cups sweetened shredded coconut

1 Basic Cake Recipe (page 12)

For the frosting
1 recipe White Mountain Frosting (page 192)

¼ cup Simple Syrup (page 198)

½ cup sweetened shredded coconut

Prepare the pastry cream and place it in the refrigerator to set.

Preheat the oven to 350°F and position a rack in the center. Grease and flour two 9-inch round cake pans.

Spread the coconut evenly on a baking sheet and toast 8 to 10 minutes, until lightly browned, with some white spots. Place on a rack to cool.

When it is cool, grind the coconut in a food processor until fine, about 30 seconds.

Prepare the cake batter according to the recipe, with the following change: In Step 1, add the ground coconut to the flour mixture.

Divide the batter between the prepared pans. Bake for 15 to 20 minutes, until the edges pull back from the pans and a toothpick inserted in the center of the cakes comes out clean. Cool the cakes in the pans on a rack.

While the cakes are cooling, prepare the frosting.

When the cakes are cool, run a knife around the edges of the pans and turn the cakes out onto the rack. Place one of the layers on a cake stand or plate. Use a pastry brush to lightly moisten the top of the layer with about 2 tablespoons of the simple syrup. Spread the pastry cream in an even layer on the cake, leaving a ⅛-inch border around the edge (the pastry cream will spread when you put the second layer on top). Moisten the top of the second cake layer with the remaining simple syrup. Place the second layer upside down on top of the pastry cream.

Frost the cake with the frosting (see page 9 for step-by-step illustrations). Cover the cake with the coconut, sprinkling it in an even layer across the top and using your hand to gently press it onto the sides.

Chill for at least 1 hour, or up to 48 hours, before serving.

Creamsicle Cake

Here we transform a favorite ice cream dessert into a cake. There's something about those two flavors that people just love (think Orange Julius too). The acidity of the orange is cut by the creaminess of the vanilla—in this case, orange cake layered with rich vanilla pastry cream and topped with orange buttercream. Greg has often used this combination on dessert menus (see Orange Vanilla Baked Alaska, page 129). **Serves 10 to 12**

For the filling

1 recipe Pastry Cream (page 187)

For the cake

*Baking spray with flour or unsalted butter and
all-purpose flour for the pans*

1 teaspoon grated orange zest

1 Basic Cake Recipe (page 12)

For the frosting

1 recipe Buttercream (page 190)

1 tablespoon orange zest

3 tablespoons Simple Syrup (page 198)

1 tablespoon Triple Sec or other orange-flavored liqueur

Prepare the pastry cream and place it in the refrigerator to set.

Preheat the oven to 350°F and position a rack in the center. Grease and flour two 9-inch round cake pans.

Combine the orange zest with the sugar for the cake in a food processor and process until well blended; the mixture will resemble wet sand.

Prepare the cake batter according to the recipe, using the orange sugar.

Divide the batter between the prepared pans. Bake for 15 to 20 minutes, until the edges pull back from the pans and a toothpick inserted in the center of the cakes comes out clean. Cool the cakes in the pans on a rack.

When the cakes are cool, run a knife around the edges of the pans and turn them out onto the rack.

Prepare the buttercream. Add the orange zest and mix on high speed until fully combined.

Combine the simple syrup and Triple Sec in a small bowl and stir until combined.

Place one of the layers on a cake stand or plate. Use a pastry brush to lightly moisten the top of the layer with about 2 tablespoons of the syrup. Spread the pastry cream in an even layer on the cake, leaving a ⅛-inch border around the edge (the pastry cream will spread when you put the second layer on top). Moisten the top of the second cake layer with the remaining syrup. Place the second cake upside down on top of the pastry cream.

Frost the cake with the orange buttercream (see page 9 for step-by-step illustrations).

Chill for at least 2 hours, or up to 48 hours, before serving.

Elvis's Favorite

Legend has it that the King loved the combination of peanut butter and bananas. Though he supposedly liked them grilled in a sandwich, we combine them in a cake. **Serves 10 to 12**

For the cake

*Baking spray with flour or unsalted butter and
 all-purpose flour for the pans*

1 Basic Cake Recipe (page 12)

2 very, very ripe medium bananas, pureed (to yield about 1 cup)

For the filling and frosting

1 recipe White Mountain Frosting (page 192)

1 cup creamy peanut butter

2 ripe but not mushy medium bananas, sliced into ¼-inch disks

Preheat the oven to 350°F; position a rack in the center. Grease and flour two 9-inch cake pans.

Prepare the cake batter according to the recipe, with the following change: In Step 5, add the warm milk and butter to the banana puree, stir until combined, and then add to half the batter. Stir quickly but gently until the banana puree is evenly distributed. Gently fold the banana batter into the remaining batter until completely combined and no streaks remain.

Divide the batter between the prepared pans. Bake for 15 to 20 minutes, until the edges pull back from the pans and a toothpick inserted in the center of the cakes comes out clean. Cool the cakes in the pans on a rack.

While the cakes are cooling, prepare the frosting, and leave it in the mixing bowl. Combine the peanut butter with ¼ cup hot water and stir until smooth. Add the peanut butter mixture to the frosting and mix on high speed until combined.

When the cakes are cool, run a knife around the edges of the pans and turn the cakes out onto the rack. Place one cake on a cake stand or plate. Spread one-third of the frosting evenly on the cake. Arrange the sliced bananas on the frosting evenly; press down slightly so they sink into the frosting. Place the second cake upside down on the bananas. Frost the cake with the remaining frosting (see page 9 for step-by-step illustrations). Chill for at least 1 hour, or up to 48 hours, before serving.

German Chocolate Cake

Originally known as German's Chocolate Cake, this cake is not, as many people think, from Germany. It takes its name from the sweet chocolate baking bar created by Sam German for Baker's chocolate company right here in the United States in 1852. The first published recipe for the cake appeared in 1957 in a Dallas newspaper. Though you can still buy German chocolate (the apostrophe and the *s* were dropped over the years), we prefer the stronger flavor of semisweet chocolate. This is not intended to be perfect looking—you want to see a few drips of filling down the sides. **Serves 10 to 12**

For the cake

Baking spray with flour or unsalted butter and all-purpose flour for the pans

1 Basic Cake Recipe (page 12)

6 ounces semisweet chocolate, chopped

For the filling and frosting

½ cup shredded sweetened coconut

1 cup chopped pecans

One 14-ounce can sweetened condensed milk

4 tablespoons (½ stick) unsalted butter

1 large egg yolk

¼ cup Simple Syrup (page 198)

Preheat the oven to 350°F and position a rack in the center. Grease and flour two 9-inch round cake pans.

Prepare the cake batter according to the recipe, with the following change: In Step 5, melt the chocolate in a large bowl in the microwave, or melt the chocolate in a double boiler and then transfer it to a large bowl (this must be done at the last minute so the chocolate doesn't set). Add the warm milk and butter to the chocolate and stir until combined, then add the chocolate to half of the batter. Stir quickly but gently until the chocolate is evenly distributed. Gently fold the chocolate batter into the remaining batter until completely combined and no streaks remain.

Divide the batter between the prepared pans. Bake for 15 to 20 minutes, until the edges pull back from the pans and a toothpick inserted in the center of the cakes comes out clean. Cool the cakes in the pans on a rack. Leave the oven on.

While the cakes are cooling, prepare the filling: Spread the coconut and pecans together in an even layer on a baking sheet, and toast until the coconut is lightly browned, with some white spots, and the nuts are aromatic, 7 to 9 minutes. Place on a rack to cool.

Combine the condensed milk, butter, and yolk in a medium saucepan over medium heat. Cook, stirring constantly (taking care to scrape the sides and bottom of the pan), until the mixture thickens to the consistency of mayonnaise and just shows signs of simmering at the edges, about 4 minutes. Remove from the heat and add the toasted coconut and pecans. Cool in the pan for 5 minutes before assembling the cake.

When the cakes are cool, run a knife along the edges of the pans and turn them out onto the rack. Place one of the layers on a cake stand or plate. Use a pastry brush to lightly moisten the top of the layer with about 2 tablespoons of the simple syrup. Spread about one-third of the filling in an even layer on the cake, leaving a ⅛-inch border around the edge (the filling will spread when you put the second layer on top). Moisten the top of the next cake layer with the remaining simple syrup. Place the second layer upside down on top of the filling, pressing gently so that some of the filling oozes out the sides.

Spoon the remaining filling onto the center of the top of the cake. Using the bottom of an offset spatula, spread the filling from the center to the edges of the cake, letting some drip over the sides.

Serve while the frosting is still warm, or serve at room temperature.

Gingerbread Caramel Apple Cake

The concentrated caramel applesauce has an intense flavor strong enough to stand up to the fragrant gingerbread spices. Apples are one of the few fresh fruits available during winter, and this hearty cake takes full advantage of them. **Serves 10 to 12**

For the cake

Baking spray with flour or unsalted butter and
*   all-purpose flour for the pans*

1 Basic Cake Recipe (page 12), minus ½ cup of the granulated sugar

2 teaspoons ground ginger

½ teaspoon ground cinnamon

¼ teaspoon ground allspice

¼ cup unsulphured molasses

½ cup packed dark brown sugar

For the filling and topping

1½ cups sugar

3 pounds Granny Smith apples (about 6 medium), peeled,
*   cored, and cut into 1½-inch pieces*

1 recipe Whipped Cream (page 197)

Cinnamon for garnish

Preheat the oven to 350°F and position a rack in the center. Grease and flour two 9-inch round cake pans.

Prepare the cake batter according to the recipe, with the following changes: In Step 1, add the ginger, cinnamon, and allspice to the flour mixture. In Step 2, add the molasses to the warm milk and butter. In Step 3, replace ½ cup of the granulated sugar with the dark brown sugar.

Divide the batter between the prepared pans. Bake for 15 to 20 minutes, until the edges pull back from the pans and a toothpick inserted in the center of the cakes comes out clean. Cool the cakes in the pans on a rack.

While the cakes are cooling, prepare the filling: Spread the sugar in an even layer in a dry 12-inch stainless steel skillet over high heat. Cook the sugar, without stirring, until about two-thirds of it has melted and turned a light amber color, 3 to 5 minutes. Stir to combine— the stirring will cause the remaining sugar to melt. Add the apples; the caramel will seize. Cover, reduce the heat to low, and cook for 5 minutes. Remove the lid, increase the heat to medium-high, and cook, stirring occasionally to break up clumps of caramel, until the apples are soft and have completely absorbed the caramel, 10 to 15 minutes. Remove from the heat.

Prepare the whipped cream.

When the cakes are cool, run a knife along the perimeter of the pans and turn the cakes out onto the rack. Place one of the layers on a cake stand or plate. Spread the hot filling in an even layer right to the edges. Top with the second layer of cake and press down so that filling oozes out of the sides slightly, then use the edge of an offset spatula to scrape the sides of the cake so the filling is even with the cake.

Spread the whipped cream on top of the cake in an even layer. Sprinkle with cinnamon. Refrigerate for 1 hour before serving.

Lemon Meringue Cake

Here we take all the best components of our favorite diner pie and transform it into a cake. This cake is stunning—the golden peaked meringue is sure to impress your guests. Unfortunately, it doesn't hold well, so be sure to make it just before serving. **Serves 8**

For the filling

1 recipe Lemon Curd (page 185)

For the cake

Baking spray with flour or unsalted butter and
  all-purpose flour for the pans

1 Basic Cake Recipe (page 12)

For the meringue

5 large egg whites

⅔ cup sugar

Prepare the lemon curd and place it in the refrigerator to set.

Preheat the oven to 350°F and position a rack in the center. Grease and flour two 9-inch round cake pans.

Prepare the cake batter according to the recipe.

Divide the batter between the prepared pans. Bake for 15 to 20 minutes, until the edges pull back from the pans and a toothpick inserted in the center of the cakes comes out clean. Cool the cakes in the pans on a rack.

When the cakes are cool, run a knife around the edges of the pans and turn the cakes out onto the rack.

Heat the oven to 375°F.

Prepare the meringue: Mix the egg whites in a large bowl with an electric mixer at medium speed until frothy, about 1 minute. Slowly add the sugar, then increase the speed to high and whip the meringue to stiff peaks (see page 7), 2 to 3 minutes.

Place one of the cake layers on an ovenproof cake plate or greased cookie sheet. Spread the lemon curd in an even layer on the cake, leaving a ¼- inch border around the edge (the pressure of the second layer will spread the curd to the edges). Place the second layer upside down on top of the curd.

Using a metal icing spatula, apply the meringue thickly and evenly over the cake. Using the tip of the spatula, pull up small peaks of meringue all over the top and sides of the cake. Bake the cake until the meringue is evenly browned, 6 to 8 minutes.

Serve immediately.

Margarita Cake

Okay, we know: it sounds weird. But trust us. This cake is delicious and incredibly festive. All the components of a classic margarita are here: tequila buttercream, lime curd, Triple Sec simple syrup. Don't worry, you won't get tipsy from this cake. But feel free to enjoy a real margarita on the side. You can make the lime curd up to 3 days ahead. **Serves 8 to 10**

For the filling

1 recipe Lime Curd (page 185)

For the cake

*Baking spray with flour or unsalted butter and
    all-purpose flour for the pans*

1 Basic Cake Recipe (page 12)

For the frosting

1 recipe Buttercream (page 190)

3 tablespoons tequila

3 tablespoons Simple Syrup (page 198)

1 tablespoon Triple Sec or other orange-flavored liqueur

Prepare the lime curd and place it in the refrigerator to set.

Preheat the oven to 350°F and position a rack in the center. Grease and flour two 9-inch round cake pans.

Prepare the cake batter according to the recipe.

Divide the batter between the prepared pans. Bake for 15 to 20 minutes, until the edges pull away from the pans and a toothpick inserted in the center of the cakes comes out clean. Cool the cakes in the pans on a rack.

While the cakes are cooling, prepare the frosting. Make the buttercream. Add the tequila and mix on high speed until fully combined.

Combine the simple syrup and Triple Sec in a small bowl.

When the cakes are cool, run a knife around the perimeter of the pans and turn the cakes out onto the rack. Place one of the layers on a cake stand or plate. Use a pastry brush to lightly moisten the top of the layer with about 2 tablespoons of the syrup. Set aside ½ cup of the lime curd for garnish. Spread the remaining lime curd in an even layer on the cake, leaving a ⅛-inch border around the edge (the curd will spread when you put the second layer on top). Moisten the top of the second cake layer with the remaining syrup. Place the layer upside down on top of the curd.

Frost the cake with the tequila buttercream (see page 9 for step-by-step illustrations). Top the cake with the reserved lime curd, spreading it into a circle and leaving a ¼-inch border around the edge.

Chill for at least 2 hours, or up to 48 hours, before serving.

Milk Chocolate Mousse Cake

Remember the gooey chocolate birthday cake you loved as a kid? Well, here's the grown-up version. It's not as rich as some chocolate cakes, or as sweet, but the smooth, silky buttercream, the moist chocolate cake, and just the hint of mocha in the mousse will make this a grown-up birthday party standard. **Serves 10**

For the cake
Baking spray with flour or unsalted butter and all-purpose flour for the pans

1 Basic Cake Recipe (page 12)

¼ cup cocoa, whisked to remove lumps

For the filling and frosting
1 recipe Milk Chocolate Mousse (page 186)

1 recipe Chocolate Buttercream (page 190)

¼ cup Simple Syrup (page 198)

Preheat the oven to 350°F and position a rack in the center. Grease and flour two 9-inch round cake pans.

Prepare the cake batter according to the recipe, with the following change: In Step 1, add the cocoa to the flour mixture.

Divide the batter between the prepared pans. Bake for 15 to 20 minutes, until the edges pull back from the pans and a toothpick inserted in the center of the cakes comes out clean. Cool the cakes in the pans on a rack.

Meanwhile, prepare the mousse and buttercream.

Line a 9-inch cake pan with plastic wrap, leaving plenty of overhang. (When the cake is finished, you will use the plastic wrap to remove the cake from the pan.)

When the cakes are cool, run a knife around the edges of the pans and turn the cakes out onto the rack. Place one of the cake layers in the prepared cake pan. Use a pastry brush to lightly moisten the top of the layer with about 2 tablespoons of the simple syrup. Pour the mousse on top of the cake, and spread it in an even layer. Moisten the top of the next cake layer with the remaining simple syrup. Place the layer syrup side down on top of the mousse. Pull the edges of plastic wrap over the top of the cake to cover, and refrigerate for at least 2 hours, or up to 48 hours.

After the cake has set, unmold it: Peel back the plastic, place a plate over the pan, and invert the cake onto the plate. Pull down on the plastic wrap as you lift up the cake pan and remove it. Gently remove the plastic wrap.

Frost the cake with the chocolate buttercream (see page 9 for step-by-step illustrations).

Chill for at least 2 hours, or up to 48 hours, before serving.

Orange Pecan Praline Cake

Named for the French duke of Plesslis-Praslin (the second part of the name is pronounced prawlin), the first pralines were made in the seventeenth century. They were brought by French settlers to Louisiana, where pralines have become part of the culture. Somewhat similar to pecan brittle, pralines are sweet and crunchy—great in this cake, paired with the pungent acidity of oranges (or on their own as a sinful snack). And, by the way, in New Orleans it's still "praw-lin," never "pray-line." **Serves 10 to 12**

For the praline

1 cup pecan halves

2 cups confectioners' sugar

For the cake

*Baking spray with flour or unsalted butter and
    all-purpose flour for the pans*

1 Basic Cake Recipe (page 12), minus the granulated sugar

½ cup packed dark brown sugar

For the filling and frosting

1 recipe Buttercream (page 190)

1 tablespoon grated orange zest

3 tablespoons Simple Syrup (page 198)

1 tablespoon Triple Sec or other orange-flavored liqueur

Grease a cookie sheet with baking spray or butter. Combine the pecans and sugar in a medium skillet over medium-high heat. Stir constantly until the sugar is completely melted and turns a deep toffee color. Pour the praline onto the greased cookie sheet and allow it to set, about 15 minutes.

Preheat the oven to 350°F and position a rack in the center. Grease and flour two 9-inch round cake pans.

Break the cooled praline into small pieces and grind it in a food processor until it resembles wet sand, about 25 seconds.

Prepare the cake batter according to the recipe, with the following changes: In Step 1, add ½ cup of the ground praline to the flour mixture. In Step 3, omit the granulated sugar and add the dark brown sugar to the eggs and yolks.

Divide the batter between the prepared pans. Bake for 15 to 20 minutes, until the edges pull back from the pans and a toothpick inserted in the center of the cakes comes out clean. Cool the cakes in the pans on a rack.

When the cakes are cool, run a knife around the edges of the pans and turn the cakes out onto the rack.

Prepare the buttercream. Add the orange zest and ¼ cup of the ground praline and mix on high speed until fully combined.

Combine the simple syrup and Triple Sec in a small bowl and stir to blend.

Place one of the cake layers on a cake stand or plate. Use a pastry brush to lightly moisten the top of the layer with about 2 tablespoons of the syrup. Spread one-third of the buttercream in an even layer on the cake, leaving a ⅛-inch border around the edge (the buttercream will spread when you put the second layer on top). Moisten the top of the next cake layer with the remaining syrup. Place the second layer upside down on top of the buttercream.

Frost the cake with the remaining buttercream (see page 9 for step-by-step illustrations). Press the remaining ground praline onto the sides of the cake (not only does this look nice, it will hide any smudges or mistakes!).

Chill for at least 2 hours, or up to 48 hours, before serving.

Raspberry Rye Cake

At the venerable Café des Artistes in New York City, there is a dessert cart with a daily changing selection of European-style desserts. One of the desserts that doesn't change is the raspberry rye torte. This is Greg's take on that combination, which may sound odd but is quite delicious. It is common to use stale bread instead of flour in European desserts, and in Greg's version, ground rye bread is used in place of some of the flour. The cake doesn't taste like rye bread, but it does have a mysterious and slightly savory spice. The jam makes the cake moist (like toast and jam!), and the final sprinkle of cinnamon ties it all together. **Serves 10 to 12**

For the cake

Baking spray with flour or unsalted butter and all-purpose flour for the pans

6 large or 8 small slices seedless rye bread

1 Basic Cake Recipe (page 12)

For the filling and topping

½ cup seedless raspberry jam

1 recipe Whipped Cream (page 197)

½ teaspoon ground cinnamon

Preheat the oven to 350°F and position a rack in the center. Grease and flour two 9-inch round cake pans.

Toast the bread in the oven on a baking sheet (it will dry out more there than in the toaster) until very dry and crisp, about 12 minutes. Break the bread into pieces and grind in a food processor until very fine, about 30 seconds. You should have 1 cup of crumbs (since the size of rye bread varies from brand to brand, you may have to adjust the number of slices to get 1 cup of crumbs).

Prepare the cake batter according to the recipe, with the following change: In Step 1, use only ¼ cup flour, and add the rye crumbs to the flour mixture.

Divide the batter between the prepared pans. Bake for 15 minutes, or until the edges pull back from the pans and a toothpick inserted in the center of the cakes comes out clean. Cool the cakes in the pans on a rack.

When the cakes are cool, run a knife around the edges of the pans and turn the cakes out onto the rack. Place one of the layers on a cake stand or plate. Spread the jam in an even layer on the cake, right to the edge. Place the second layer upside down on top of the jam.

Refrigerate until ready to serve, up to 24 hours.

Up to 2 hours before serving, prepare the whipped cream and spoon it onto the center of the cake. Using an offset spatula, spread the whipped cream in an even layer to the edges of the cake. Garnish with the cinnamon, and refrigerate until ready to serve.

Snickers Cake

The malt flavor of Ovaltine (a classic powdered milk drink perhaps more remembered for the secret decoder rings it gave away) is reminiscent of the nougat in a Snickers bar, and the salty peanuts combined with the sweet milk chocolate frosting is really what a Snickers bar is all about: that great sweet-salty combination. This cake isn't as cloyingly sweet as a Snickers bar—though, unfortunately, it's not as portable either. **Serves 10 to 12**

For the cake

Baking spray with flour or unsalted butter and
  all-purpose flour for the pans

1 Basic Cake Recipe (page 12)

¾ cup Ovaltine powder

For the filling and frosting

1 recipe White Mountain Frosting (page 192)

8 ounces milk chocolate, chopped

½ cup salted peanuts, finely chopped

Chopped peanuts for garnish (optional)

Preheat the oven to 350°F and position a rack in the center. Grease and flour two 9-inch round cake pans.

Prepare the cake batter according to the recipe, with the following change: In Step 2, stir the Ovaltine into the warm milk and butter until dissolved.

Divide the batter between the prepared pans. Bake for 15 to 20 minutes, until the edges pull back from the pans and a toothpick inserted in the center of the cakes comes out clean. Cool the cakes in the pans on a rack.

When the cakes are cool, run a knife around the edges of the pans and turn the cakes out onto the rack.

Prepare the frosting. Melt the chocolate in a small bowl in the microwave, or melt the chocolate in a double boiler. Let it cool slightly. Combine the frosting, melted chocolate, and peanuts in the bowl of a stand mixer and mix on high speed until fully combined.

Place one of the cake layers on a cake stand or plate. Spread one-third of the frosting in an even layer on the cake. Place the second layer upside down on top of the frosting. Frost the cake with the remaining frosting (see page 9 for step-by-step illustrations). Garnish with chopped peanuts, if desired.

Chill for at least 1 hour, or up to 48 hours, before serving.

Strawberry Mousse Cake

This is our more grown-up version of strawberry shortcake. A beautiful cake, with a row of perfect strawberries around the side, it makes a great dinner party dessert.

Don't wash the berries, or they will get soggy; just wipe off any visible dirt with a damp paper towel. **Serves 10 to 12**

For the cake

Baking spray with flour or unsalted butter and all-purpose flour for the pans

1 Basic Cake Recipe (page 12)

For the filling

¼ cup Simple Syrup (page 198)

10 to 12 nice evenly sized strawberries, wiped clean

1 recipe Strawberry Mousse (page 189)

Confectioners' sugar

Preheat the oven to 350°F and position a rack in the center. Grease and flour two 9-inch round cake pans.

Prepare the cake batter according to the recipe.

Divide the batter between the prepared pans. Bake for 15 to 20 minutes, until the edges pull back from the pans and a toothpick inserted in the center of the cakes comes out clean. Cool the cakes in the pans on a rack.

Line a 9-inch cake pan with plastic wrap, leaving plenty of overhang on the sides. (When the cake is finished, you will use the plastic wrap to remove the cake from the pan.)

When the cakes are cool, run a knife around the perimeter of the pans and turn them out onto the rack. Place one cake layer in the prepared pan, right side up. Brush the top of the cake with about 2 tablespoons of the simple syrup. Hull and halve the strawberries, and arrange them around the perimeter of the pan with the cut side facing in, alternating berries with the point down and the point up so they fit snugly together. Trim the berries if necessary so they are even with the top rim of the pan. Set aside.

Prepare the mousse.

Pour the mousse into the prepared pan, spreading it in between the strawberries as much as possible. Brush the remaining simple syrup on the top of the second cake layer and place it upside down on top of the mousse. Press down gently, and pull the plastic wrap over the top to cover. Place another 9-inch cake pan on top of the cake to weight it and refrigerate until set, at least 4 hours, or up to 48 hours.

After the cake has set, unmold it: Peel back the plastic wrap, place a plate over the pan, and invert the cake onto the plate. Pull down on the plastic wrap as you lift up the cake pan and remove it.

When ready to serve, gently remove the plastic wrap and sprinkle the cake with confectioners' sugar. When slicing, be sure to cut in between the strawberries for easier cutting and nicer slices.

Tiramisu Cake

You might think that tiramisu has a rich and storied history in Italy, but in fact this popular dessert was born in the 1960s, in Treviso. It spread like wildfire, however, and today can be found on menus at Italian restaurants across the globe. Here's another take on a recent classic; we substitute coffee-flavored sponge cake for the espresso-soaked ladyfingers but still use the traditional Marsala and zabaglione, the Italian egg custard. **Serves 8 to 10**

For the cake

Baking spray with flour or unsalted butter and all-purpose flour for the pans

1 Basic Cake Recipe (page 12)

1 tablespoon instant coffee

For the filling and topping

⅓ cup dry or sweet Marsala

4 large egg yolks

3 tablespoons sugar

1 recipe Whipped Cream (page 197)

8 ounces mascarpone, at room temperature

2 tablespoons Simple Syrup (page 198)

2 tablespoons brewed coffee

2 tablespoons dark rum

Grated chocolate, optional

Ground cinnamon

Preheat the oven to 350°F and position a rack in the center. Grease and flour two 9-inch round cake pans.

Prepare the cake batter according to the recipe, with the following change: In Step 3, stir the coffee into the warm milk and butter mixture until it is dissolved.

Divide the batter between the prepared pans. Bake for 15 to 20 minutes, until the edges pull back from the pans and a toothpick inserted in the center of the cakes comes out clean. Cool the cakes in the pans on a rack.

While the cakes are cooling, prepare the filling: Fill a large bowl halfway with ice, and set aside. Combine the Marsala, egg yolks, and sugar in a large bowl set over a pot of barely simmering water. Whisk constantly and vigorously (find a strong friend to help you) until the mixture goes from frothy to thick and light and holds its shape (it will look like the cake batter), 2 to 3 minutes. Remove from the heat, set the bowl in the bowl of ice, and continue to whisk until the zabaglione is cool to the touch (it will continue to thicken slightly and will resemble soft whipped cream when done), 2 to 3 minutes longer.

Prepare the whipped cream. Reserve half of it to top the cake (keep it in the refrigerator). Gently mash the mascarpone in a large bowl. Add one-third of the remaining whipped cream and stir gently to combine. Add the remaining whipped cream in two batches, stirring until just combined; mascarpone is very fragile and will break if overworked. Add the Marsala-egg mixture in two batches, gently folding in each addition until smooth.

Combine the simple syrup, coffee, and rum in a small bowl. When the cakes are cool, run a knife around the edges of the pans and turn the cakes out onto the rack. Place one of the layers on a cake stand or plate. Brush the top of the cake with about 3 tablespoons of the syrup. Spread the filling in an even layer on the cake, right to the edges. Brush the top of the second cake layer with the remaining syrup. Place the second layer syrup side down on top of the filling. Press down gently so that some of the filling oozes out the sides.

Chill for at least 1 hour, or up to 24 hours before serving.

Up to 1 hour before serving, spoon the reserved whipped cream onto the center of the cake. Using an offset spatula, spread the cream in an even layer to the edges of the cake. Garnish with grated chocolate, if desired, and ground cinnamon just before serving.

Fillings, Frostings, and Toppings

We suggest particular fillings and frostings for the individual cakes, but feel free to mix and match your favorite flavors. Any of the mousses can make a great dessert on its own, or combine two of them—how about Dark Chocolate Mousse and Strawberry Mousse? Most of the fillings and frostings would be good on any simple chocolate or vanilla cake. And Simple Syrup? Well, let's just say we won't rest until there's a jar of simple syrup in every refrigerator in the country.

Champagne Granita

Granitas are an easy way to make a frozen dessert at home without an ice cream maker. Just freeze and stir. And stir. And stir. This low-tech approach makes the texture of a granita coarse and grainy, not smooth like a sorbet—which does require an ice cream maker. **Makes about 3 cups**

1 bottle Champagne or sparkling wine

½ cup sugar

Combine the Champagne and sugar in a medium saucepan over medium-high heat and bring to a boil. Cook until reduced to 3 cups, 5 to 7 minutes. Pour into a shallow baking dish and place in the freezer immediately.

After 1 hour, check to see if the mixture has begun to ice over. If it has, run a fork back and forth through the mixture several times to break up ice pieces. Repeat every half hour until the granita is granular and frozen, 2 to 3 hours.

Dark Chocolate Mousse

This mousse is denser and easier to make than an egg-based chocolate mousse. That density allows it to hold its shape well, making it easy to slice and serve a mousse cake. Take care to fold the ingredients together as quickly but gently as possible. Whipping the cream adds lots of air and volume to it, and overworking it when adding the chocolate will allow all that air to escape. Because there are so few ingredients in this mousse, the flavor of the chocolate really stands out; the better the chocolate, the better the mousse. **Makes 2¹/₂ cups**

6 ounces semisweet chocolate, coarsely chopped

2 tablespoons unsalted butter

3 tablespoons brewed coffee, dark rum, or water

1 cup heavy cream

Bring a small pot of water to a gentle simmer. Combine the chocolate, butter, and coffee in a medium heatproof bowl that can sit atop the pot without touching the water. Place the bowl over the pot and stir until the chocolate and butter are just melted and the mixture is smooth. Remove from the heat and set aside.

Whip the cream at high speed to soft peaks (see page 7), about 1 minute.

Fold one-quarter of the cream into the chocolate until combined but not fully incorporated and some streaks remain. Repeat with the remaining cream, mixing to fully incorporate when adding the last quarter.

If you are going to use the mousse in Double Chocolate Mousse Bombe (page 120), use it right away, when it is still quite soft. If you want to use it in a pie, pour the mousse directly into the prepared crust. If you want to serve it on its own, you can pour it into dessert dishes to set or leave it in the bowl to scoop when you're ready to serve. Refrigerate until set, at least 2 hours, or up to 48 hours.

Vanilla Ice Cream

Okay, we're realistic: we know that most people wouldn't dream of making homemade ice cream. Thankfully, you don't have to; there are now dozens of good-quality ice creams on the market. But for those of you who do make your own, here is a simple recipe that can be the base for any number of flavors, not just the ones in the cake recipes in this book. To create your own flavors, fold in your favorite candies, cookies, or any kind of flavoring when the ice cream is still soft, right out of the ice cream maker.
Makes 2 quarts

2 cups whole milk

4 cups heavy cream

8 large egg yolks

1 cup sugar

2 teaspoons vanilla extract

Heat the milk and cream in a medium saucepan over medium heat until hot but not boiling. Remove from the heat.

Whisk together the yolks and sugar in a medium heatproof bowl. Add a small amount of the hot milk to the yolks (about ⅓ cup) and whisk to combine. Slowly add the remaining milk and whisk to combine.

Place the bowl over a pot of barely simmering water. Cook the custard, stirring frequently and slowly, until thickened, about 15 minutes; you should be able to trace your finger through the egg mixture on the spatula and leave a track. Refrigerate until cold to the touch, about 30 minutes.

Stir in the vanilla. Pour the custard into your ice cream machine and follow the manufacture's instructions. This may need to be done in two batches, depending on the machine's capacity. Transfer the ice cream to a freezer container and freeze.

Lemon Curd

English in origin, lemon curd is a custard made with lemon juice rather than milk or cream. In England it's often served as a preserve with biscuits and other jams at afternoon tea, but here it is best known as lemon meringue pie filling. Curds in your curd?—don't worry. If little white curds form in your curd, it's just a little scrambled egg; pass the curd through a medium strainer before adding the zest, and no one will be the wiser.

Press the plastic wrap directly onto the surface of the curd to prevent a skin from forming as it cools. **Makes 3 cups**

3 large eggs

3 large egg yolks

¾ cup fresh lemon juice (from about 4 lemons)

¾ cup sugar

8 tablespoons (1 stick) unsalted butter, cut into 8 pieces

1 tablespoon grated lemon zest

Whisk together the eggs and yolks in a small bowl, and set aside.

Bring a small pot of water to a simmer. Combine the lemon juice, sugar, and butter in a medium heatproof bowl that fits over the pot without touching the water. Place the bowl over the water and stir occasionally until the butter is melted and the sugar is dissolved. Whisking constantly, slowly add the eggs in a steady stream to the lemon mixture. Continue to whisk constantly and vigorously until the mixture is thickened and the whisk leaves tracks in the curd, 3 to 5 minutes.

Remove from the heat and add the lemon zest. Place plastic wrap directly on the surface of the curd and refrigerate until cold, at least 1 hour, or up to 1 week.

Lime Curd: Substitute lime juice for the lemon juice and lime zest for the lemon zest.

Milk Chocolate Mousse

One of the best things about this mousse is that it's very simple, with only a handful of ingredients and few steps. Yet the mousse is so versatile—not to mention so tasty—you'll soon find yourself whipping some up to fill a graham cracker crust for chocolate mousse pie, or to serve on its own, topped with some fresh raspberries for an elegant dessert. Or you could just eat it right out of the bowl with a soupspoon, as we do.

Be careful when combining the chocolate and the whipped cream. Whipping the cream adds lots of air and volume to it, and overworking it when adding the chocolate will allow all that air to escape (and then you'll have chocolate sauce, not mousse). **Makes 2 cups**

2 tablespoons brewed coffee

5 ounces milk chocolate, coarsely chopped

1 tablespoon dark rum (optional)

¾ cup heavy cream

Bring a small pot of water to a gentle simmer over medium heat. Combine the coffee, chocolate, and rum, if using, in a medium metal bowl that can sit atop the pot of water without touching the water. Place the bowl on the pot and heat until the chocolate is melted, stirring often. When the mixture is smooth, remove from the heat and set aside to cool until no longer warm to the touch.

Whip the cream at high speed to soft peaks (see page 7), about 1 minute.

Fold half of the cream into the chocolate until combined but not fully incorporated and some streaks remain. Add the remaining cream in two batches, mixing to fully incorporate when the last batch is added.

If you are going to use the mousse in Milk Chocolate Mousse Cake (page 169), use it right away, when it is still quite soft. If you want to use it in a pie, pour the mousse directly into the prepared crust. If you want to serve it on its own, you can pour it into dessert dishes to set or leave it in the bowl to scoop when you're ready to serve. Refrigerate until set, at least 1 hour, or up to 48 hours.

Pastry Cream

Pastry cream is better known to most cooks as vanilla custard or pudding. It's great in other desserts but also good on its own. Press the plastic wrap directly on the surface of the pastry cream to prevent a skin from forming as it cools. **Makes 3 cups**

2 cups milk

6 large egg yolks

¼ cup cornstarch

⅓ cup sugar

1 teaspoon vanilla extract

Heat the milk in a medium saucepan over medium heat until hot but not boiling. Remove from the heat.

Combine the egg yolks, cornstarch, and sugar in the bowl of a stand mixer fitted with the whisk attachment and mix on high speed until thickened and light, about 2 minutes. When you lift the whisk, the mixture should fall back on itself like a ribbon.

Add half of the hot milk to the egg mixture and mix to combine. Slowly add the egg mixture to the remaining hot milk (still in the saucepan), whisking constantly. Heat over medium-high heat, stirring slowly and constantly and taking care to scrape the sides and corners of the pan (so it won't scorch), until the pastry cream is thickened, about 2 minutes. When the pastry cream begins to thicken (you will see some small lumps form), reduce the heat to low and mix vigorously and constantly, beating out the lumps, until it is smooth and as thick as pudding (a few small lumps may remain), about 2 minutes longer. Bring to a boil, stirring constantly; since the cream is so thick, it won't boil like water but will "breathe" large bubbles to the surface when you stop stirring. Continue to cook 10 to 15 seconds longer.

Transfer to the clean bowl of the stand mixer fitted with the clean whisk and mix on high speed until steam stops rising out of the bowl, about 2 minutes. Add the vanilla and mix 1 minute longer. Transfer to a bowl and press plastic wrap directly on the surface of the cream. Refrigerate until cold and set, at least 1 hour, or up to 48 hours.

Coconut Pastry Cream: Substitute ½ cup coconut milk for ½ cup of the milk.

Peanut Butter Mousse

This mousse isn't too sweet, and the cream cheese adds a nice tang. Try serving it layered with Milk Chocolate Mousse (page 186) in parfait glasses. **Makes 2 cups**

8 ounces cream cheese, at room temperature

1/2 cup creamy peanut butter

1/2 cup heavy cream

1/4 cup sugar

Using the whisk attachment on your mixer, whip the cream cheese on high speed until fluffy, 3 to 5 minutes, stopping once to scrape down the sides of the bowl. Add the peanut butter and mix on low speed until just combined, taking care not to deflate the cream cheese. Transfer the mixture to a medium bowl, and clean the mixer bowl.

Whip the heavy cream and sugar together at high speed to soft peaks (see page 7). Add one-third of the whipped cream to the peanut butter mixture and gently stir until combined. Add half of the remaining whipped cream and fold gently until no streaks remain; repeat with the remaining cream. Refrigerate until set, at least 1 hour, or up to 48 hours.

Strawberry Mousse

Fruit mousses too often taste gummy and artificial. This one is light and fluffy, and it holds its shape without being rubbery. The better the strawberries, the better the mousse—so make this only when the strawberries are in season. **Makes 3 cups**

4 cups (about 1 quart) strawberries, hulled and quartered

1 packet (2½ teaspoons) gelatin

½ cup sugar

1 cup heavy cream

Puree the strawberries in a food processor until smooth, about 30 seconds. Press the puree through a medium strainer to remove the seeds. You should have 2 cups puree. Set aside.

Sprinkle the gelatin over 3 tablespoons warm water in a medium heatproof bowl. Set over a pot filled with 1 inch of gently simmering water. The gelatin will absorb all the water at first and seem gummy, but as it is heated, it will melt and liquefy. Once it has liquefied, add ½ cup of the strawberry puree and stir over the heat until smooth.

Remove from the heat, add the remaining strawberry puree and the sugar, and stir to combine. Refrigerate until just beginning to set, 10 to 15 minutes.

Once the strawberry mixture is set, whip the cream to soft peaks (see page 7). Add half of the cream to the strawberry mixture and stir to combine. Add the remaining whipped cream and gently fold to combine.

If using the mousse as a filling, use it immediately, before it sets completely. If serving it on its own, divide it among individual dessert dishes or pour into a large serving dish and refrigerate until set, at least 4 hours, or overnight.

Buttercream

Greg used to make a classic American buttercream—butter, confectioners' sugar, and raw egg yolks—but due to growing health concerns about raw eggs, he decided to create one with cooked eggs. For this recipe, you make a custard (cooked eggs, milk, and sugar) and work in lots of air and butter. The buttercream is easy to make, but it has an incredible silken texture. And it's not as sweet as some other buttercreams. It keeps well in the fridge for 4 to 5 days or can be frozen in a plastic container for up to 1 month. If making this for a recipe that calls for only half of the amount, prepare the entire recipe and freeze the rest for another cake. **Makes 2 cups**

3 large egg yolks

2 tablespoons milk

½ cup sugar

*½ pound (2 sticks) unsalted butter, each stick
    cut into 8 pieces, at room temperature*

Place the egg yolks, milk, and sugar in a small pot over medium heat. Cook, stirring constantly, until the mixture is foamy and hot, about 2 minutes. Pass the mixture through a medium strainer to remove any lumps, then transfer to the bowl of a stand mixer fitted with the whisk attachment and beat on high speed until the mixture is cool (when the bottom of the bowl is cool, the mixture inside should be cool, but you should stick your finger in to be sure—after turning the mixer off, of course), about 6 minutes.

With the mixer on medium speed, slowly add the butter one piece at a time, mixing thoroughly after each addition. The buttercream will be smooth, shiny, and fluffy.

Buttercream is easiest to work with at this stage: soft, slightly loose, and very spreadable. Once refrigerated, the buttercream will harden (like butter!) and be impossible to spread. But you can bring the buttercream back to a spreadable consistency by slowly warming it in a metal bowl set over a pot of gently simmering water, or by softening it in the microwave at 50 percent power for about 30 seconds. Once the buttercream begins to soften, transfer it to the bowl of a stand mixer and beat on low speed until smooth and pliable.

Chocolate Buttercream: Add 4 ounces semisweet chocolate, melted and cooled slightly, to the buttercream while it is still in the mixer and mix on high speed until fully combined and no streaks remain.

Cream Cheese Frosting

Have all the ingredients at room temperature, and this frosting will be a snap. If you happen to have any left over, it can be held in the refrigerator for 4 to 5 days or frozen for 1 month. Though it's standard on Carrot Cake (page 152), it's also good on Gingerbread (page 26). **Makes 2½ cups**

½ pound (2 sticks) unsalted butter, each stick
cut into 4 pieces, at room temperature

1 pound cream cheese, cut into 4 pieces, at room temperature

1 cup confectioners' sugar, whisked to remove lumps

1 tablespoon vanilla extract

Using the paddle attachment, beat the butter in a stand mixer on medium speed until very light and fluffy, like whipped cream, about 1 minute. Add the cream cheese one piece at a time, mixing well after each addition. When all the cream cheese is incorporated, slowly add the sugar and then the vanilla. Mix just enough to remove any lumps.

If the frosting seems thin, refrigerate until just slightly firm before frosting a cake.

White Mountain Frosting

We wanted a foolproof white fluffy frosting, and we had almost given up. Our initial efforts came out grainy, loose, or flat, and we were just about ready to throw in the towel when we turned to our collection of antique cookbooks and found inspiration in Meta Given's *Modern Encyclopedia of Cooking*. With just a few modifications, we had the frosting of our dreams: luxurious, satiny, shiny white fluff. **Makes 3 cups**

½ cup sugar

¼ cup corn syrup

2 large egg whites

Pinch of salt

½ teaspoon vanilla extract

Combine the sugar, corn syrup, and 2 tablespoons water in a small saucepan over medium-high heat. Stir occasionally until the sugar is dissolved. Bring to a boil and cook until the syrup reaches the soft ball stage: when you drop a bit in some cold water, it forms a soft ball that does not dissolve (235°F). Cover and remove from the heat.

Whip the egg whites and salt at high speed in the bowl of a stand mixer to soft peaks (see page 7). Turn the mixer off and add the syrup, then mix at high speed until cool; the frosting will be thick, stiff, and like Marshmallow Fluff. Add the vanilla and mix until combined. Use immediately.

Caramel Glaze

Many caramel recipes require a candy thermometer, but Greg finds them bothersome and hard to read, so he doesn't use one. There are other reliable ways to tell when caramel is ready. Cooking the glaze to the soft ball stage (about 235°F) means that when you drop a bit in some cold water, it forms into, yes, a soft ball and does not dissolve; if it does dissolve, continue cooking the caramel, change the water, and try again in 30 seconds or so. The glaze is almost ready when it becomes shiny and smooth and the bubbles go from light and frothy to tight and dense. Don't stir the caramel once all the ingredients are combined; stirring disrupts the caramel and will cause crystallization (crunchy bits of sugar in the caramel). **Makes ¾ cup**

1 cup packed dark brown sugar

4 tablespoons (½ stick) unsalted butter, cut into 4 pieces

¼ cup heavy cream

Combine all the ingredients in a medium saucepan over medium-high heat. Stir constantly until the butter is completely melted and the sugar is dissolved. Bring to a boil, without stirring, and cook until the mixture reaches the soft ball stage, 1 to 2 minutes; when you drop a bit in some cold water, it does not dissolve. Remove from the heat and transfer to a bowl. Use immediately.

Caramel Frosting (makes 1 cup): Place the hot glaze in the bowl of a stand mixer fitted with the paddle attachment and mix at high speed until the bowl is cool to the touch, stopping twice to scrape down the sides, 10 to 12 minutes. With the mixer running, add 2 tablespoons softened unsalted butter and mix until combined. Use immediately.

Chocolate Glaze

Too many chocolate glazes are cloyingly sweet and rich, especially when paired with sweet cake and fillings. We prefer to use a combination of semisweet and unsweetened chocolate. This is wonderfully shiny; refrigeration, however, will cause it to lose that shine. Some of the shine will return as the glaze returns to room temperature, but it will never get as shiny as it once was so, whenever possible, leave glazed cakes at room temperature.

The glaze hardens as it dries, making it a perfect dip for fresh fruit, like whole bananas or strawberries, or as a topping for ice cream. Any extra glaze can be stored in the refrigerator and then melted in a double boiler or in the microwave as needed. **Makes 1 cup**

4 tablespoons (½ stick) unsalted butter, cut into 4 pieces

2 ounces semisweet chocolate, chopped

2 ounces unsweetened chocolate, chopped

¼ cup corn syrup

Bring a small pot of water to a gentle simmer. Combine all the ingredients in a heatproof bowl that can sit atop the pot without touching the water. Place the bowl over the pot and stir until the ingredients are just melted and combined. Use immediately.

Hot Fudge Sauce

Though most often paired with ice cream, whipped cream, and a cherry, hot fudge has the potential for so much more. It's at home at the breakfast table, drizzled over Belgian waffles or French toast, and it can be used to make an intensely rich chocolate milk shake. Or, for a grown-up milk shake, make a Mudslide: combine some hot fudge, Kahlúa, and ice cream. You can even use this hot fudge as fondue, serving it with cubes of pound cake, chunks of banana, and strawberries. **Makes 1½ cups**

4 ounces semisweet chocolate, chopped

¼ cup cocoa powder, whisked to remove lumps

4 tablespoons (½ stick) unsalted butter, cut into 4 pieces

½ cup sugar

¼ cup corn syrup

Combine all of the ingredients with ½ cup water in a medium saucepan over medium heat. Cook, stirring often, until the chocolate and butter melt and the mixture is smooth. Bring to a boil, reduce heat to low, and simmer until slightly thickened, about 10 minutes.

Let the hot fudge cool slightly before using—you want hot fudge, not scalding fudge. You can leave it at room temperature for 20 to 30 minutes, or, if you just can't wait, throw it in the freezer for about 5 minutes.

Store the hot fudge in an airtight container in the fridge for up to 3 months or in the freezer for up to 6 months. Reheat the sauce in a microwave or over low heat.

Strawberry Sauce

All you need for an easy, beautiful sauce are some strawberries and a jar of jam. **Makes 1½ cups**

4 cups (about 1 quart) strawberries, hulled and quartered

1 cup strawberry preserves

2 tablespoons fresh lemon juice

Combine all the ingredients in a medium saucepan over medium-high heat and bring to a boil, stirring occasionally. Reduce the heat to low and simmer until the sauce is thickened and the berries are soft, 3 to 5 minutes. Serve cold or at room temperature.

Whipped Cream

When whipping fresh cream, chilling the bowl makes a big difference; the colder the cream, the easier it will be to incorporate air. Even if you don't have an electric mixer, whipping cream is not difficult or time-consuming: recruit your guests to help, and have them take turns whisking the cream by hand. **Makes 3 cups**

1½ cups heavy cream

2 tablespoons sugar

½ teaspoon vanilla extract

Refrigerate the bowl and whisk until cold, about 10 minutes (if you're in a rush, fill the bowl with ice water for a couple of minutes; be sure to dry the bowl thoroughly before adding the cream). Add all the ingredients to the bowl and whip at high speed to soft peaks (see page 7), about 1 minute. Use immediately.

Flavored Whipped Cream: Add 2 tablespoons flavoring to the cream before whipping it. Here are some of our favorites: rum, brandy, Frangelico (hazelnut liqueur), amaretto (almond), and kirsch (cherry).

Chocolate Whipped Cream: Stir ½ cup cocoa powder (whisked to remove lumps) into the cream before whipping it.

Simple Syrup

True to its name, this recipe is probably the easiest to prepare in this book. Once you've made a batch to keep in your fridge, you'll wonder how you ever lived without it. Not only does it make cakes moist, it also adds sweetness to cold drinks without leaving a crunchy sugar residue at the bottom (perfect for iced coffee) and it forms the base for sorbet. When you're ready to use it in a cake, pour just the amount needed into a small bowl—you'll likely get crumbs in the syrup and will have to discard any unused portion. We recommmend always keeping a jar of simple syrup in the fridge, especially during the summer iced-coffee and lemonade season (not to mention the year-round margarita season).

Equal parts sugar and water (i.e., 1 cup sugar, 1 cup water)

Place the sugar and water in a small saucepan and stir together. Bring the mixture to a boil, stirring often to prevent the sugar from separating to the bottom. Let the mixture boil for 3 minutes without stirring. Remove from the heat and cool before using. Keep refrigerated in an airtight container until ready to use.

Index

F

fennel semolina raisin bars, 89

fig ouzo cake, 25

fillings, frostings, and toppings, 181–98

    buttercream, 190

    caramel glaze, 193

    Champagne granita, 182

    chocolate glaze, 32–33, 194

    cream cheese frosting, 191

    dark chocolate mousse, 183

    decorative swirl in, 10

    frosting techniques, 8–10

    hot fudge sauce, 195

    lemon curd, 185

    milk chocolate mousse, 186

    pastry cream, 187

    peanut butter mousse, 188

    simple syrup, 198

    strawberry mousse, 189

    strawberry sauce, 196

    vanilla ice cream, 184

    whipped cream, 197

    White Mountain frosting, 192

folding ingredients, 7

fool, apricot parfaits, 78–79

frangipane petits fours, 90–91

frosting, technique, 8–10

frostings, *see* fillings, frostings, and toppings

frozen desserts:

    bluberry coffee cake terrine, 122–23

    lemon soufflé cake, 124–25

    orange vanilla baked Alaska, 129–30

    root beer float ice cream cake, 133–34

    vanilla ice cream, 184

G

German chocolate cake, 161–62

ginger:

    apricot cake, 144

    gingerbread, 26

    gingerbread caramel apple cake, 163–64

    peach upside-down cake, 65–66

glazes:

    caramel, 193

    chocolate, 32–33, 194

    white, 32–33

Grand Marnier orange upside-down cake, 64

granita, Champagne, 182

H

hazelnut chocolate roulade, 118–19

honey:

    nut upside-down cake, 58

    sesame cake, 27

hot fudge:

    sauce, 195

    upside-down cake, 59

hot milk sponge cake, 11

    basic recipe, 12–13

I

ice cream:

    orange vanilla baked Alaska, 129–30

    root beer float cake, 133–34

vanilla, 184
individual berry shortcakes, 92–93

J

jelly and peanut butter upside-down cake, 67
jelly roll, 126

K

key lime cheesecake, 28–29

L

layer cakes, 143–80
  apricot ginger, 144
  Black Forest, 145–46
  Boston cream pie, 147–48
  cappuccino, 149–50
  caramel, 151
  carrot, 152–53
  cassata, 154–55
  coconut cream, 156–57
  creamsicle, 158–59
  Elvis's favorite, 160
  German chocolate, 161–62
  gingerbread caramel apple, 163–64
  lemon meringue, 165–66
  margarita, 167–68
  milk chocolate mousse, 169–70
  orange pecan praline, 171–72
  raspberry rye, 173–74

Snickers, 175–76
  strawberry mousse, 177–78
  tiramisu, 179–80
leavening, 11
lemon:
  coconut roulade, 127–28
  meringue cake, 165–66
  poppy seed cake, 30
  soufflé cake, frozen, 124–25
lemon curd, 185
lime:
  curd (note), 185
  key, cheesecake, 28–29
liqueurs:
  Black Forest cake, 145–46
  chocolate cherry caramel upside-down cake, 53–54
  creamsicle cake, 158–59
  dulce de leche upside-down cake, 57
  fig ouzo cake, 25
  margarita cake, 167–68
  orange Grand Marnier upside-down cake, 64
  orange pecan praline cake, 171–72
  strawberry bombe, 137–38
  trifle, 141–42

M

macadamia nut pineapple cake, 38
madeleines, butterscotch, 94
maple:
  cranberry upside-down cake, 60
  walnut cake, 31
marble cake, 32–33
margarita cake, 167–68
Mexican chocolate cake, 34